Gaslighting Recovery
Workbook

How to Recognize Manipulation, Overcome Narcissistic Abuse, Let Go, and Heal from Toxic Relationships

indirect, that are incurred as a result of the use of the information contained within this document, including, but not limited to, errors, omissions, or inaccuracies.

Table of Contents

Your Free Gift

As a way of saying thanks for your purchase, I want to offer you a free bonus e-Book called *7 Essential Mindfulness Habits* exclusive to the readers of this book.

To get instant access, just go to:

https://theartofmastery.com/mindfulness

Inside the book, you will discover:

- What is mindfulness meditation?

- Why mindfulness is so effective in reducing stress and increasing joy, composure, and serenity
- Various mindfulness techniques that you can do anytime, anywhere
- 7 essential mindfulness habits to implement starting today
- Tips and fun activities to teach your kids to be more mindful

Introduction

Take a moment to imagine this situation.

You've been arguing with a friend or partner about something. This "something" could be something small or something big, but whatever the topic of conversation, the other person has made you feel, well, a little confused and manipulated. Maybe even left you doubting yourself and as though things weren't as they seemed, even if you were sure they were. This is a form of abuse known as gaslighting.

This confusion could come to you in several different ways. Perhaps that person has made you feel emotional and played on an insecurity you have, heightening how you feel while fully knowing what they are doing and how they make you feel. Maybe you've been convinced that something happened, or you felt a certain way when something tells you deep down that this isn't the case.

This has been a reoccurring situation throughout my life. I had it with my father, an abusive man who treated my mother and me the same. I found similar things happen in some friendships, as well as romantic relationships. I've heard stories of it happening in the workplace and among grandparents. Allow me to share a straightforward example.

Let's say you're with someone and you agreed you were going to have a date night on Friday. Friday night comes around, and you get yourself ready, and suddenly they say, "Oh no, I said Saturday night. I'm busy tonight. Silly you!"

It's crucial to note that this doesn't mean that your partner is gaslighting you in this case. Perhaps they did tell you the wrong day, or you genuinely misheard them and got the days wrong. That does happen from time to time. The problems start to arise when this becomes a regular occurrence.

I'm going to cut straight to the point. Gaslighting is a form of control. You might think, *Why would someone bother lying about something so small like what day date night was or what their favorite takeout is?* but it all comes down to one simple premise.

Control.

Take a moment to ask yourself, is there anyone around you who continually makes you anxious, or leaves you feeling the need to always apologize, or even makes you question your sanity? Think about it; does any of this sound familiar? This situation may be gaslighting coming to play. Gaslighting overrides your reality to the extent that you begin to question your judgment.

In a relationship, putting someone down and making them feel like they either aren't paying attention to what's being said or making them feel like they're stupid or silly because they're not able to remember things correctly is a way of putting someone down and holding the back of their foot. The person being gaslighted feels shame for not being good enough, and this can make them want to try harder and harder, thus making the person doing the gaslighting even more in control of the situation.

Is this starting to ring any bells?

Whether you've heard of gaslighting before, been recommended this book or a similar book, or you've experienced these situations yourself, this is your first reminder that you don't have to live this way. Being manipulated by somebody in your life, which can be in any form of a personal or professional relationship, is not okay, and you don't need to put up with it.

However, I want to slow things down right now and take things back to the beginning. Throughout this book, we're going to explore everything you need to know about gaslighting, including what it is, where it comes from, how you can spot it, how you can avoid it, and most importantly, how you can get out of a gaslighting situation.

We're going to be covering everything throughout the following chapters. While initially focusing on gaslighting, including topics like what it is, where it comes from, and signs you can look out for, we'll also dive into toxic relationships of all kinds, how you can spot them, how to deal with them, and sharing advice on how to get out of them.

At the end of every chapter, I've included the workbook aspect of this book, giving you a few writing prompts that you can fill out in the book or your own writing space, whether in your diary, journal, or on the Notes app on your phone. Whatever feels safe and comfortable to you.

These prompts will help you guide your mind into identifying what kind of abuse you're experiencing and what you can look out for in your relationships. It then all comes together to give you the mindset and information you need to actionably deal with the abuse, and provides you with suggestions on what to do next.

Anyway, you'll see what I mean as you start making your way through the book, but just so we're all on the same page, let's get right down to the basics.

The History of Gaslighting

Perhaps surprisingly, the term gaslighting has been around for quite some time. The idea first appeared in a stage play from 1938 known as *Gas Light,* a mystery thriller written by the British playwright

Patrick Hamilton. There were also film adaptions produced in both 1940 and 1944.

The plot of the screenplay is relatively simple. The main husband in the play sets out to convince his wife, and others in his life, that she is insane and does so by changing, manipulating, and controlling their home and the overall environment in which they live.

Of course, the wife is not insane, so when she questions why things are slightly different, he attempts to persuade her that she is wrong, delusional, or has a poor memory. Going by the play's name, the most common way he does this is by slowly dimming their home's gaslights and then pretending there has been no change.

There's a more in-depth plotline to this that follows the idea that he killed a woman and is looking for her lost jewelry. Getting his wife assessed and placed in a mental institution will allow him to search more effortlessly and become her power of attorney.

But like the meaning of the term today, gaslighting is all about getting control over someone in a manipulative and emotionally destructive way. Imagine someone who has been subject to these kinds of practices for several years and how they will feel about themselves. Perhaps, like me, you don't need to imagine too hard.

Since the play and movies came out, clinicians and laypeople have utilized gaslighting to depict psychopathic conduct. There's no denying that acting in such a way is a cruel act of using psychological efforts to confuse and question someone's reality or rational soundness. It is a severe form of psychological mistreatment that frequently drives the victim to ask whether the memories, thoughts, or situations they've experienced are actually true.

As we'll describe throughout this book as the "gaslighter," the person who performs this manipulative mental strategy can take advantage of this vulnerable state of mind by providing the victim with false information to be perceived better. The gaslighter then has full control over the victim, forcing them to believe whatever narrative they want them to believe.

Abuse comes in numerous forms, and it does not segregate as a result of race, sex, religion, or sexual orientation. The consequential damage from any form of abuse can be physical, mental, emotional, sexual, financial, and many more—usually a combination of several. Being yelled at, hit, threatened, or always chided are brief examples of abuse. Having sex or withholding money are also ways people can get abused. These are the more obvious forms of violence. The problem is, excluding individual circumstances, these forms of abuse are relatively easy to spot and notice. Gaslighting, on the other hand, is not.

In many cases, some of which we'll explore throughout this book, the victims are often so overwhelmed by the perpetrator's behavior and the feeling of self-doubt that comes as a result of this that it may take a long time to realize what is happening and ultimately seek the necessary support.

Gaslighting abuse affects thousands, if not hundreds of thousands of people worldwide, and it's one that remains very close to my heart. As a mother of two kids, I have had up close and personal experiences with gaslighting. I struggled in a toxic relationship for close to ten years, an intimate relationship that I justified in my head over and over again, no matter what happened. One day I was able to open my eyes and finally saw how my relationship for what it was.

Guess who? It was my first husband, and this was my worst experience by far. The abuse was intensely psychological, as it often is, to generate suspicions in my mind to truly brainwash me. I was doggedly loyal to the marriage, as you would be when you're married to the supposed love of your life, but he was an excellent liar. In hindsight, I knew he was a compulsive liar from the beginning, but I always thought that I would be the one to change him into a better person, and I loved him, so I accepted him just the way he was. It was my lot in life to be with him, love him, and give myself to him. Ah, the innocence of love, hey?

I'll share my specific experiences with you in a bit more detail as we cover each section throughout the book, but I'll start with this and take a moment to see if it sounds familiar. My misplaced trust in my husband and my relationship caused me to question myself at every move and on every little thing. I would often apologize to him for my "craziness." I lost my self-esteem and sense of identity. I was on the verge of losing my sanity as the situations I'd find myself in had an enormous effect on my beliefs, reality, and psychology.

However, as soon as I was introduced to gaslighting and other similar forms of psychological abuse, I got educated and started to see what was actually happening within my relationship and how I wasn't treated right. I soon realized I had allowed myself to get conned. Eventually, I decided it was time to leave the marriage, but it took me quite a while to get back to some degree of mental and emotional equilibrium.

Gaslighting is not just a one-time event or temporary, but it continues indefinitely until the light shines on the situation. In fact, the more it occurs, the worse the effects become. It's like a snowball effect. The more it happens, the less self-esteem the victim has and the more controlling the perpetrator becomes. A hallmark of this mental and emotional abuse is concealment, and with it, gaslighting keeps flourishing.

A story that pulled at my heart and was one of the stories that inspired me to write this book was one told to me by a lady called Grace. Grace (not real name) had a sister, Terry (also not real name), who has been undermining her life, spirit, and responsibilities for decades.

Terry's abuse initially started with vicious gossip and backbiting, and as it gained increased strength daily, it escalated rapidly. She got more recruits to her cause of discounting her sister, which increased her power and control. As often and thoroughly as Terry could, she needed to show that power. She regularly made efforts to convince everyone that her sister, Grace, was delusional about family matters and just the reality of life in general, and that their mother had full dementia.

Terry planned to put their mother in a care facility against her will. In essence, this was to "get finished with her." Her words, not mine. It was clear from conversations and even text messages that Terry was very interested in the family land that her mother still owned, and their mom's presence was blocking that. As a result of Terry's initial constant abuse of their mom, Grace remained living in fear. However, as the abuse towards her mother worsened, Grace joined the efforts to block their mom's transition to the care facility, and the focus of Terry shifted from her mother to Grace herself. She became the target.

This happened in numerous ways, but in hindsight, it's easy to see that it could have been passed off as nothing since the actions were so subtle. Grace later shared that it was the not-so-subtle actions that gave it away. For example, if Grace's mother forgot what she was doing or simply couldn't remember a simple piece of information, Terry would explode about this clearly being dementia, and their mother would be better off at home.

Maybe this is something a worried daughter would say on a one-off occasion, perhaps followed by something like "Oh, we should probably get you a doctor to see if anything is going on" if it was a genuine concern. However, when everyone is relentlessly told that something is wrong, this creates serious doubt in the victims' minds.

When Terry got friends and family members on her side, this only fueled the fire, and it would be complicated to get out of. Relentless and unforgiving, both their mother and Grace felt what Terry was up to.

Immediately after the attention shifted focus, Grace's mental status, and even the way she did things in her life, began to undergo questioning. Both Grace and their mother kept living in the fears that Terry caused. Eventually, their mom passed on, and Grace became the open target. Terry continued shaking the mental health and emotional stability of her sister. In one extreme situation, Terry even stabbed herself and threw down the knife to say it was her sister, Grace, who did it. Grace found out later that Terry had announced to the family that she was delusional and hooked on pills. The gaslighting was indeed advanced in her case. However, in the end, Grace recovered from this dark disorder and got balanced mentally and emotionally with external supports, and was able to free herself from having Terry in her life.

According to the most up-to-date research, gaslighting can occur in any relationship. In most cases, the gaslighters are relatively close to their victims, which is the exact reason why it can be so powerful, regardless of whether it is on personal or professional terms. It is a common strategy used by abusive spouses or intimate partners, narcissists, and individuals who attempt to monitor large groups of people like cult leaders. The results are often devastating. Although this appears to be a difficult technique and seems highly sophisticated, it has sadly become an ordinary happening in all kinds of relationships. It may be the husband who tells his wife she's imagining things to cover up an affair, the boss who denies in public the help for a project she vowed to get in private. It may even be the specialist who changes his story from one visit to the next, telling the patient that he "never said that," which are mostly instances of gaslighting in action in real life.

This mental manipulation, especially if it has an emotional attachment to it, is veiled, subtle, and operates on deep emotional levels. These manipulations also cause the victims to find means to defend themselves, but slowly, this mental abuser has a way of striking at the victim's verdict. At first, the victim becomes confused as they realize something is not right and attempts to speak to the abuser about what they have discovered. However, the abuser will disprove the victim's discoveries, convincing him or her (the victim) with the idea that they are wrong and the abuser is somewhat right. Although this may seem insignificant at first, with consistency and regular situations, the victim gradually loses control and begins to doubt his or her thinking. The effects start to snowball from here.

It's worth noting again at this point, just for clarity, that if someone gaslights another person in a one-off instance, saying something like "Oh, you're just imagining things, don't be silly," then this perhaps isn't gaslighting. This kind of psychological abuse comes from long-term implications in all manners of situations, but maybe scarily can occur both consciously and unconsciously.

The trick is to notice the signs of it happening and then do something about it. This could be leaving the relationship you're in, getting the support and help you need to build up your self-confidence and self-esteem once again, and then moving forward with your life. In other situations, it could mean sitting down with your partner and having a hard conversation, perhaps even attending some kind of therapy.

As the title implies, this book, *Gaslighting Recovery Workbook,* aims to help you recover from the gaslighting situations you may have found yourself. This book is broken down into several parts that involve helping you understand what gaslighting is (covering a little bit of the scientific side to what we've discussed already), including the stages it comprises of, the signs to look out for that indicates someone is trying to gaslight you, the conventional techniques employed, and what effects gaslighting can have on the victim.

We're also going to explore how you can find out who narcissists are, what this means, their various types, how they implore gaslighting methods, variations of emotional and psychological abuse, their effects, and gaslighting in relationships, be it personal or professional. Most importantly, this book tells you how you can deal with current or the impact of past gaslighting situations, heal from them, and regain your lost sense of identity and self-worth. *Gaslighting Recovery Workbook* will also help place you in your right frame of mind without any coercion or force at play as you read through.

Therefore, if you suspect that you are getting gaslighted in your relationship(s), this book is a must-read for you. Ready to start working on recovering from gaslighting today?

Let's get right into it.

Chapter One

What is Gaslighting?

"I am mad. I'm always losing things and hiding things, and I can never find them. I don't know where I've put them." - Paula Alquist Anton

Gaslighting is a metaphorical term that refers to mental abuse in a manipulative form. Often, the abuser will present false information to their victims so they will be perceived better.

For example, if person A has text messages from a woman he is having an affair with, he might try to hide them so his wife doesn't find out. Let's say his wife sees a text message on his phone from a girl called Tessa. She might say, "Who's Tessa? I saw a message from her on your phone." Person A might reply with something like, "What message? I don't know anyone called Tessa." He might delete the message to prove there are no messages. When this happens, Person B, in this case, the wife, may doubt whether she even saw the message at all, when really, she did. Thus, she's being manipulated into believing a lie and is doubting herself and her truth incorrectly.

According to Dr. Robin Stern (2011, para 9), he defines gaslighting as a systematic attempt by someone to erode another's reality by telling them that the things they are experiencing are not so. The abuser's goal is to make their victims unsure about their memory and sanity over a particular situation, turning against their cognition, emotions, and who they are (Stern 2019, para 3).

This way, the victims do not see the abuser as having done anything wrong, but it is, in fact, them that have the problem and are seeing things incorrectly. It is a form of psychological abuse that gets used to instill in a victim an extreme sense of anxiety and disarray to the extent that they do not trust their memory, judgment, or perception. This psychological warfare is both a deliberate and systematic approach between an abuser (the gaslighter) and the victim (the gaslightee). Anyone can be a victim of this gaslighting abuse, regardless of gender, age, race, or intelligence. There is no barrier to it.

The Source

In the introduction, the 1944 Hollywood classic movie *Gaslight*, directed by George Cukor, featured Ingrid Bergman as the wife, Paula, and Charles Boyer as her cunning husband, Gregory. The film took place in Victorian England, starting with the murder of Alice Alquist in London. Alice was a famous opera singer who was incredibly wealthy throughout her career. Additionally, Alice had raised her niece, Paula, since her childhood after her biological mother's death. After Alice's death, Paula was sent to Italy to study opera from her Aunty Alice's old teacher. While studying in Italy, she met a good-looking older man named Gregory Anton, and together they had a great romantic relationship and got married soon after.

Some time passes, and Gregory persuades Paula to return to live in London with him in a house that her aunt has willed to her. Upon their arrival, Paula found a letter from a man called Sergius Bauer addressed to her aunt hidden in a book. The letter was written two days before the murder occurred. On seeing the message, Gregory reacted violently but quickly regained his composure and later justified his outburst as angry at seeing his lovely wife trying to bring back to life saddening memories.

Once Alice's belongings were removed from the attic, Gregory's diabolical psychopathic behavior became strikingly out of the ordinary. He systemically and deliberately drives Paula crazy by psychologically deceiving the things around her in secret. In his endeavors to control her, he started to monitor her condition in a manner that made her inquire about her rational soundness. He achieved this by controlling different components in their typical state and afterward insisting his wife is not right when she takes a stab at recalling how the elements were initially.

Don't let these explanations put you off. While this all may sound a bit complicated, I'm using how scientists and psychologists talk about these kinds of abusive situations, so you know what you're dealing with. A more straightforward and perhaps more relatable way of talking about this, especially concerning the movie, is whenever a picture on the wall is missing in Gregory and Paula's home, Gregory convinces her that she changed it, even when she does not have any memory of doing so.

As gas was used for the lighting fixtures in the home, using gas lamps as many homes in that era did, the term gaslighting originated from the scene where the husband uses the gaslights to search for the hidden jewels as soon as he gains entry into the attic. Whenever he creeps upstairs and turns on the attic lights, the gaslights continue to dim in the remaining part of the house accordingly since it was all connected to one main system. At other times, Gregory would dim the gas lights with diabolical psychological technique, making them flicker and deny anything was going on whenever his wife, Paula, referenced it. He would reveal to her she was insane and that everything was going right with them. One quote, in particular, stands out.

"Why don't you rest for a while?" Gregory suggested. "You know you have not been well."

As viewers and audience members, we know this to be incorrect. Gregory is purposefully manipulating Paula, so he has full control over her, crushing her self-esteem as the movie progresses and causing her to doubt herself and her sound state of mind.

Over time, through the consistency and repetition of Gregory's techniques, Paula actually begins to believe that she is going mad. Gregory almost succeeds in his attempt to have her certified as insane and institutionalized, allowing him the opportunity to search the home for the jewels freely. He successfully isolates her from those within the house, fires Paula's trusted elderly maid, and replaces her with a younger one (Nancy), which he can easily control seductively. He stops visitors from coming to the house and never allows her to leave the house with the claim that it was all for her good as she has "kleptomania and imaginations which are due to her nervous dispositions."

The enthusiastic injury she encountered was extreme. Gregory tells everyone she was unstable, separates her from her family, and disguises cutting invalidations as statements of concern. Notice how in every situation, Gregory is making himself out to be the hero of the story. He's saving Paula, or he's saving her family from having to deal with her since "she's become insane," and he is taking care of everything on their behalf, as though he is doing them a favor. Sometimes, he even hides her possessions, and whenever she can't find them, he questions her sanity. Gregory cruelly convinces her she is losing her memory and further demoralizes her with the conviction that she has inherited her biological mother's bad genes, having known she died while insane. With a collection of abusive techniques, including deception, seduction, rejection, bullying, and isolation, Paula reluctantly agrees she is losing her mind. Therefore, she became utterly dependent on her husband for her sense of reality.

At long last, Paula got the help of an avid admirer of her aunt, Inspector Brian Cameron of Scotland Yard (performed by Joseph Cotten), and the old maid that Gregory fired. She was convinced she was not losing her psyche and that the occasions were occurring and not a result of her creative mind. She also discovered that Gregory is not who she had known him to be; he is the one who murdered her aunt, Sergius Bauer, from the letter. He had only seduced her into marrying him to gain entry into the house in London and have Alice's jewels to himself. At the end of the movie, Gregory got arrested just as he located the long-lost treasures he had been searching for throughout the movie.

Typically, especially in Gregory's case, as we've been discussing, gaslighting is performed by psychopaths, who are individuals who have a personality disorder typically portrayed by a lack of remorse for others and advanced antisocial behavior. These personality characteristics make it easy for these individuals (psychopaths) to control or manipulate other people without any sense of guilt or shame about what gets done. This makes sense. Many people who could or have manipulated people unconsciously find themselves feeling guilty if their actions come to light. Perhaps they said something for selfish reasons or to achieve a specific outcome, and sure, they understand it was the wrong thing to do, and they can admit that.

In many cases, the lessons have been learned. However, when it comes to psychopathic people, there is no remorse. There is no guilt. This can be a complicated subject, so we'll dive into it more later since there are many grey areas. For example, a psychopath could act sorry for their actions, but this could just be another attempt to emotionally manipulate the victim.

That being said, these abusive techniques are not just reserved for psychopaths. Regular individuals are just as susceptible to being perpetrators. There is a high tendency that they would also be implausible about doing it in the light of the fact that their non-verbal communication and facial appearances would part with it.

These gaslighters can be very persuasive liars and manipulators without giving away any hints whatsoever to their victims of the wrongs or hurt they are doing to them. Their objective is to obliterate their victims' actual views and perception of reality by creating and sharing lies that seem authentic and genuine.

The Doings of Gaslighting

Gaslighting is insidious as it plays on our worst fears, most anxious thoughts, our deepest wishes to be understood, appreciated, and loved (Stern 2007 chap. 1, para 7).

Now, I know there's been a lot to take in already. I know, I've been there at square one, and the whole concept can seem incredibly overwhelming and complicated.

There's so much to it, and with reality warped, you may find yourself asking what's real in your own situation, what's made up, and how you feel about it all. You may even be asking yourself whether you've gaslit people in your own life, either consciously or unconsciously.

All of this is okay. Just take things one step at a time and allow things to unfold. The whole purpose of this book is about getting educated, understanding the situations you're in, and then realizing how to deal with them. As great as it would be, this isn't an overnight process where you can snap your fingers, and everything will be okay. But that's also okay.

Let's start with highlighting the key points to think about, starting with the idea of what gaslighting is.

1. It squarely aims at taking a person's self-confidence, gradually whittling it away until they are left questioning whether what they experience, feel, or think is real or is some kind of fantasy that their minds have made up.

2. It confuses and disorients the victim in such a way that the perpetrator gains total control over them. The more the perpetrator can sow seeds of doubt in the victim's mind, the easier it becomes for them (the perpetrator) to make every situation attuned to their liking. There is a sure snowball effect.

3. The abuse continuously degrades a person's abilities and desires to challenge their perpetrator. Each time this is done, the goalpost is moved by these perpetrators again as they turn their arguments against them.

4. Eventually, the victim is incapacitated with fear and doubt as they are manipulated easily into doing whatever the abuser desires them to do. They, in turn, lose all their fight and become metaphorical puppets of these abusive masters.

Who are Gaslighters?

Gaslighting is a technique that is often used by:

- Narcissists

- Machiavellians

- Dictators

- Control freaks

- Cult leaders

- Ordinary individuals

Some Real-Life Examples of Gaslighting Statements

Initially, an individual may not be an abusive person, but they may gradually begin to gaslight over time. Again, sometimes gaslighting can happen unconsciously, or perhaps on a one-off occasion. However, if some of the following statements are frequently said to you, you could be a gaslighting victim.

1. "Everyone agrees with me. You are always overreacting towards everything."
2. "You see things the wrong way. You're imagining things."
3. "I don't know what you are talking about. Your claims are wrong."
4. "I do not comprehend what you're saying. You are just trying to confuse me."
5. "What you said is not true; you never remember things correctly."
6. "I cannot be listening to you. You never see things the right way."
7. "I only do it because I love you."
8. "You're imagining things; you are losing your mind."
9. "It did not happen that way. You know I'm right."
10. "You are too sensitive to everything."
11. "I feel you just love trying to throw me off track every time."
12. "Your imagination is getting the best of you. It did not happen that way."

Of course, there are variations of these statements that could happen all the time. Look out for them within your relationships.

Reasons for Gaslighting

After everything we've spoken about already, you may be wondering something, and this is something that played on my mind for a very long time.

Why is it that some individuals would go to such elaborate lengths to manipulate people?

Have you ever thought about this? What are they trying to accomplish? Is it a power struggle where they simply want to be in control? In reality, there is no rational reason why someone would choose to gaslight their victims. It's malicious and hurtful, and the world would be much better off without it.

Well, there are several reasons. Some researchers state that a perpetrator could have a genetic predisposition that causes them to enjoy the torment they cause to their victims sadistically. Suppose someone has experienced a complete lack of power, perhaps being abused as a child. In that case, they may have learned techniques and strive to regain control in their lives any way they can, ultimately becoming a cruel and malicious practice.

Additionally, taking control in such a way that we've discussed makes the abusers look like heroes to their victims or the people around their victims. As we spoke about with some of the examples previously, an abuser taking care of someone who they have convinced is insane makes them out to be a good person when they're not.

It's like a king of a country taking away all the food from everyone and holding it in his castle, only then to give it out as though he's the hero who's fixed everything. Abusers are often both the problem and the solution, but they will only ever admit to the latter. Sometimes, abusers will play out, so they seem to be the victims rather than the abusers. These actions are caused by their mental disorder, which there is, unfortunately, no cure.

These psychopaths can even choose to go for therapy and receive medications, but these things won't free them from the force in their brain that causes them to be this way. The only correct way to stop a psychopath is to place them in a controlled environment where mental health professionals can monitor their actions. Unfortunately, the vast majority of these psychopaths across the globe are not in such a situation. They reside in the natural world while blending in with everyone else.

The Stages of Gaslighting

From others' experiences throughout history, there are five main steps that abusers use to enable them to manipulate their victims. These stages are in no particular order, but a practical understanding of these stages would help you better understand what gaslighting is and identify it with ease if you find yourself in such a situation.

Stage 1 - Collection of Information

Usually, the first significant thing a perpetrator will do to their victims is to collect information about them to know them. They say knowledge is power, and this is destructively true when it comes to gaslighting. The more the abuser learns about their potential victim, the easier it becomes to manipulate them (the victim).

This can happen in all manner of ways. If the victim has tense relationships with their friends or parents, if they have financial problems or a traumatic past, these are all things that can be used and played down the line.

It is why family members of the abuser are so easily used as pawns in the game because the abuser already knows everything about them, having grown up with them. But with strangers and acquaintances, they will have to get to know their victim first by being friendly or perhaps even become intimate with them.

Stage 2 - Change of Orientation

One of the main objectives of an abuser is the desire to separate their victims from the rest of the world. Many refer to this as the "change of orientation," which means that they (the perpetrator) will disagree with everything the victim says and criticize them for how they perceive the world.

The abuser wants to get the victim to a state of mind where they no longer trust their own senses, skills, family, friends, and environment—ultimately changing the victim's perspective to suit the abuser's. The victim's whole world has to revolve around what the abuser either says or does.

Stage 3 - Creation of Fantasy World

The creation of a fantasy world is what many people refer to as the most powerful and essential technique in gaslighting. The abuser will invent a world exclusively for the victim. In the origin movie, the core fantasy world created was that Paula was insane and needed looking after (i.e., a fantasy).

The making of the fantasy world implies that the perpetrator will begin to provide the victim with false information about the world. Victims will defend these lies around other people, even if it means fighting for them. Abusers will continuously test their victims as to whether or not they still fit into their world. The victim will want to work hard to be in that world to experience the abuser's rewards.

This particular aspect of abuse relies on validation. Imagine being told you're an awful cook, over and over again. You're told your cooking is awful every day, and you should just give up, but you must carry on because it's your role in the household. However, you keep trying and learning because you want the validation of the abuser.

When someone else comes into your life, and you cook for them, they could tell you it's pretty good, and you may even disregard their compliments because you don't believe it to be true yourself. This is affirming your beliefs with the abuser, thus giving them control, even when they're not around.

Stage 4 - Incapacitation

Perpetrators will take over all of the duties and responsibilities that were initially carried out by the victim. Incapacitation could involve taking over the washing, cooking, cleaning, job, or anything else that the victim would typically do. It ensures that the victim entirely relies on the abuser in every way for everything, thus strengthening the power dynamic.

Stage 5 - Recruitment of Others

Abusers are typically psychopaths who conjure up lies on their own. However, they will often recruit others who unknowingly assist them with the lies, ultimately strengthening the stories and the victim's false reality.

These other people could be friends, classmates, neighbors, teachers, or coworkers of the victim. The abuser will provide these people with the same kinds of lies that they tell their primary victim. Since the victims have no reason to doubt what the abuser is telling them, they will likely support the lies and convince them they are real. Over time, the false reality becomes the perceived reality for everyone involved.

Of course, this sounds incredibly malicious, and frankly, when I first heard about it, I couldn't believe it to be true. Surely people can't mastermind such intricately detailed stories, like puppet masters manipulating the strings, but it's true.

When you consider that most lies and presumed truths are so seemly small and innocent, it's a buildup of these over time, backed by others' validation, that creates such a strong false reality.

Chapter Takeaway

And with that, we come to the end of the first chapter. I know we covered a lot, so you might want to go away and take some notes, reread some parts, and take a moment to reflect on the experiences and relationships in your life and how you may be subject to abuse.

Despite this book being a recovery workbook, it's hard to give precise advice because every situation is subjective and has its own details. One example of gaslighting is different from the next. However, there are some key points we covered in this chapter for you to take away and start your recovery journey with:

- o The term gaslighting refers to deliberate and systematic psychological abuse in a deceptive way.

- o It is an approach between an abuser (the gaslighter) and the victim (the gaslightee).

- o The word gaslight takes its source from a stage play that was later made into a film, showcasing the term in detail.

o It is a form of abuse that disorients, disables, and degrades the victim's abilities.

o There are mainly five stages to gaslighting, and it involves the collection of information, change of orientation, creation of a fantasy world, incapacitation, and recruitment of others.

Quick Checklist

Reflecting on your situation is a crucial part of the process. The fact you're reading this book at all means you've probably suspected you're a victim, or you've noticed some of the warning signs. Now is the time to identify the problems and clarify your situation. Look for a quiet and comfortable place that would allow for some deep thinking.

- Ask yourself the following questions and ensure you give yourself a sincere answer:

1. Do you often second-guess yourself? Yes/No

2. Do you feel like you find yourself going crazy? Yes/No

3. Do you notice someone around you that you often apologize to? Yes/No

4. Do you overwhelmingly sense that something seems wrong with you, even if you can't say what it is? Yes/No

5. Do you find it hard to make simple decisions? Yes/No

6. Do you feel confused most of the time? Yes/No

If you find that you're saying yes to many or most of these questions, you may be a gaslighting victim. Therefore, you can move to the next checklist.

- Make a table (an example is shown below) of some gaslighting situations (work, religious organization, romance relationship, parents) you find yourself in with the name of the gaslighters and others that they have enlisted into the gaslighting situation.

S/N	Gaslighting situation(s)	Gaslighter(s)	People recruited
1			
2			
3			
4			

Don't worry if you don't know what you should be writing next. Just do what you can. In the next chapter, we will be looking at the signs that showcase gaslighting in action, both the personal signs that reveal you are being gaslighted, and the signs to look out for in an individual that highlights abusive tendencies.

Chapter Two

Warning Signs and Symptoms of Gaslighting

"Gaslighting can be very insidious the longer it occurs such that initially, you may not realize you're being affected by it, but gradually you lose trust in your instincts and perceptions." - Darlene Lancer

Unfortunately, we live in a world where cruel and malicious people exist. They always have, and perhaps always will. An example of this is that you have probably watched the news or heard from families who share stories about a husband physically abusing his wife. Of course, it may be the other way around where the wife manipulates her husband to control him. Having such information, you are left wondering why the victim of such abuse got involved with the abuser in the first place.

You ask, "Why did she marry him? Why has she been staying with him all this while? Why did she not tell us about it?" And the list goes on. You may even conclude that "Some individuals do not value their lives," or "She should have been more careful before choosing to move in with him." However, gaslighting is an act that can take down anyone, and despite having some idea that something is wrong, it's so easy to overlook the reality of your own situation. After all, we only know what happens to us, and it's easy to speak up from an outsider's point of view or with hindsight.

In essence, this kind of abuse is an incredibly effective manipulation tactic. And keep in mind: this kind of abuse can be found in any setting or relationship—parent/child relationship, relative relationships, relationships with co-workers, and so on—not just in partner-to-partner relationships.

It can happen anywhere to anyone, which is why we're going to take the time to cover and discuss some signs you can look for in people's behavior that showcase their abusive tendencies. More so, I will be sharing some of the more personal signs that can reveal both an abuser and a victim.

Gaslightee Personal Signs

Do you think you are a victim of this gaslighting act? Here are some signs to look out for that can confirm this.

1. You lack joy and happiness in life

If you live under the gaslighter's constant tyranny, you can expect extremes of lethal hostility. As a victim, you go through physical and mental torture that can cause you to suffer a personality change and will definitely leave you feeling confused, lonely, frightened, and unhappy. Even if you find yourself in a situation where something exciting is about to happen, the highs won't tend to last long before you forget about it, and you find yourself back in a state of sadness and depression. Often you continue to carry these feelings even after you have escaped from the abuser.

The path of recovery takes time.

2. You pay attention to your character flaws

One of the primary objectives of the gaslighter is to make you think less of yourself. As we've explained already, this is so that you place your basic human need for validation on the abuser, ultimately giving them control over you.

Over time, the abuse changes your views of yourself and turns your general attitude toward yourself into a harmful one. You may discover that your daily contemplations, daydreams, and streams of thought are regularly turned inward as you fixate on your apparent antagonistic personality attributes. You now accept that you are naturally awful or damaged and that your imperfections make you unlikable or unlovable.

This is why a gaslighter will attempt to do all of this to make you more averse to leave them. You most likely end up imagining that nobody else would need you around them, so you feel forced to stay with the abuser forever.

3. Your confidence is nonexistent

This goes inseparably in line with the previous point mentioned, when you're in a position where you have such a low supposition about yourself that you acknowledge affront from your victimizer and yourself. You no longer trust in your capacities, and you don't accept that you merit bliss and all the positive, fulfilling, and frankly just good things that life has to offer. Therefore, you turn down the new opportunities that come your way to mingle, advance in your profession, or develop as an individual. You most likely experience uneasiness regularly because you don't feel ready to confront even the smallest of difficulties. This is a massive part of the snowball effect that this type of abuse is known for.

4. You always second-guess yourself and feel befuddled

You have so little trust in your memory and your capacity to work as a typical individual that you never stop thinking about your life experiences and how you have made mistakes or should have handled certain situations differently. For instance, let's say you're trying to put your grocery shopping away (say the oatmeal and the milk), and after some time, you are not sure if you have placed them in their usual place. Throughout the day, no matter what you're doing, you keep feeling as though you've placed the oatmeal in the refrigerator and the milk in the cupboard and continue to feel this way until you go to look.

As much as it goes hand in hand with second-guessing, confusion is what you feel towards numerous aspects of your everyday life. This confusion can be explicit to specific things or in the broader sense that your intellectual capacities aren't there at all. The abuser implies this through their words and actions. Since the abuse already makes you susceptible to their control through their manufactured lies, denial of facts and information—their committed appeals that you're insane, silly, or mad—asking yourself "what if" is not such an abstract concept.

5. Decisions are quite hard for you to make

It will come as no surprise that, at some point, you'll find it hard to make decisions on your own, even being unable to settle on even the most minute of choices without anyone else's input. There's simply that much of a lack of confidence. As you are invariably already second-guessing yourself, the abuse affects how you solve your problems and make decisions in your life. You simply do not accept you're equipped for picking the right choice accurately; thus, you consistently need to go to somebody to instruct you. Of course, if you're actually able to make a choice, you will second-guess yourself endlessly, furthering your doubt and lowering your self-esteem until you're unable to make that choice to begin with.

However, the person around you that you turn to for help, by design, is the same person gaslighting you and causing you to doubt yourself in the first place. The web of the gaslighter is akin to the disintegration of the self; as you are under the threat of continual danger, you already form a psychic bond with the victimizer to avoid the potential fragmentation of yourself. In creating that bond, you're compelled to organize yourself around the idealized desires of your abuser and surrender your authentic potential and your true self—the real you. The abuser has placed themselves in the position to provide solutions to every difficulty in your life. As a result, this makes you more subject to them and bound to remain with them since you don't have the foggiest idea of completing anything without their direction, even your ability to make your own decisions.

6. You find yourself constantly apologizing

You are under the assumption that whenever somebody is to be blamed in any situation around you, it will likely be you. You find yourself always apologizing for "never doing anything right." You may even find yourself having to apologize for your existence. Therefore, "sorry" is something you find yourself repeatedly saying, paying little mind to whether the fault is actually yours or somebody else's. It becomes a force of habit.

This constant apologizing plays directly into the hands of the gaslighter since they can abstain from assuming any liability for their activities, realizing that in the end, you will be saying "sorry" to them one way or another, regardless of what actually happened in reality. This power of making apologies quickly takes the shame off the gaslighter and automatically redirects it towards you.

7. You have the feeling of being a failure

You get the inclination that others are disappointed in you. Hell, you're disappointed in yourself. Your self-confidence has been tampered with endlessly, and you are filled with the belief that you have become so imperfect from numerous points of view, even in the eyes of complete strangers. In your psyche, you are simply not adequate on any level, and it is no big surprise you feel the need to apologize repeatedly.

8. You feel detached from the individual you were used to

In a bid to survive, you develop an unconscious defense mechanism that helps keep you safe. This can vary from person to person, so it's hard to focus on specifics. Still, it usually evolves things like backing down, continually apologizing, or pushing all your hard emotions down.

However, in doing this, you tend to lose yourself by complying, placating, and appeasing other people, specifically your abuser. Within your memories of the past, an alternate individual is inhabiting your body. An alternative you. In any case, you can't perceive yourself in them. You feel wholly separated from your past self since you see what you are currently (or, instead, what you think you are presently), and it does not correlate with who you were at that point. As it were, looking at how you used to be instead resembles glancing back at another person. A previous existence of you that was more confident and relaxed, probably happier and more at ease.

9. You rationalize the conduct of the abuser

At the point when a gaslighter carries on inadequately toward you around others, you rush to pardon them or even shield them. Your mind tells you that you merit this kind of treatment; thus, you would not want to hear a terrible word said against them. They are in the right and cannot be wrong.

As you are abused emotionally and psychologically, your body reacts to this action physically. Whenever you see the gaslighter around you, your whole body tenses up, and you don't know what to say or do next. You're on edge because you don't want to disappoint them, do or say the wrong thing, or look bad in any way from their perspective. However, it's this physical reaction of tensing up, which is a component of the human's natural flight-freeze response, as it sets your body up to prepare for incoming gaslighting.

Of course, as something that's developed over time, you may not even be aware that it's happening until you take a moment to realize and notice it for yourself. Whether you or someone you know is being abused, look for the clenching of a jaw, raised shoulders, or tension in the person's muscles.

10. You lie to yourself as well as other people to dodge confrontations

As you have gotten used to being ground down and crushed, abhorring confrontations of any sort is what you have grown accustomed to. Thus, to avoid the littlest of disagreements, you lie, say yes to things you would preferably say no to, and ultimately try to create your own false reality where everything is okay and nothing is wrong.

You agree to others' demands or requests without addressing them, or even if you don't want to out of fear of making them unhappy or push you down further. Your frequency in making apologies always, as stated in point number six, is not what you do to be polite, as is commonplace with most people.

Instead, you see apologizing as a powerful tool to stay safe while you are in your daily war zone, and you see it as a means to calm down the rage of the gaslighter. Sometimes, you may even act against your moral ethics and beliefs in circumstances just to maintain peace and avoid arguments.

11. You are wondering if you are excessively sensitive

In the first point earlier mentioned, one of the typical character flaws you may find within yourself is being overly sensitive in your attitudes. Projections and blame are the emblems of gaslighting, which takes a toll on your emotional stability, and quite rightly. However, instead of concluding that something is wrong in your life, or there is a source to your pain and suffering, you may accept that you blow up on occasion to what others might have said or to certain situations. Over time, you may start blaming your reactions to situations and events as the thing that causes a large portion of the issues you face. You become hypersensitive to the frequent humiliation the gaslighter sends your way. You'll probably hear numerous times that you are "too sensitive" and "are blowing things out of proportion."

As a result, you start looking for approval before doing anything, scared that you will make more mistakes that will end in more and more humiliation. This entire process makes you further doubt everything about yourself, so that you often ask, "Am I too sensitive?"—once again, placing the blame of what is wrong on yourself.

12. You sense something is not right, yet you can't figure out what

The gaslighter's objective is to be in charge and influence the reality of the gaslightee, which perpetuates massively when the victim has lost awareness of what is actually happening.

Where it counts, while you're by yourself, or when you're around people who aren't your abuser, you may come to realize that something about your relationship with this individual is not right, or you actually feel happy, freer, and more stable when you're not around that one person.

However, the problem remains that you cannot see the red flags evident to other people looking in from the outside. You are not sure what the issues are; thus, you do not have the foggiest idea of addressing them. You will also consistently have this pestering inclination that it may be you who is at fault for the sad state of things, which meets up with the gaslighter's desire.

Once again, since you have so much self-doubt, you may not even trust your judgment enough to come up with a reliable and meaningful conclusion, despite your gut feeling telling you that something is wrong.

13.You withhold information from others

It's utterly normal to experience great shame about your situation as a victim. Whether you know you are a victim or not, the feeling that something is wrong and the constant pushing down of your self-esteem is going to get to you, and frankly, it's exhausting. You feel tired of covering up this abuse as you move on. When your good friends and family members who want the best for you speak to you that you are being abused, or ask if something is wrong, of course, you don't want to spend any more time on it, so you tend to avoid the subject, and soon you learn how to withhold divulging more information to prevent further conflict.

However, the importance of shame in the abuse of a gaslighter is problematic because of the snowball effect it has. While talking about what you're going through with people who care is one of the hardest things to open up and do, it's also one of the most beneficial.

When attempting to open up about what you've been through, the shame you face is a normal response to the social failure that victims often feel due to the abuse—that is to say, the shame of being unable to protect yourself from the misuse in the first place. This shame can be seen as defensiveness and withdrawal by others, pushing these well-meaning friends and family members away, or ultimately allowing you to slip into a place where you don't want to open up because the shame is too much.

Of course, these signs to look out for can be complicated and individual in their own way. Some abusers may gaslight mainly using other people's influence, whereas others may be very personal and direct. It's sometimes easier to focus on what makes an abuser and then couple all the signs to see if they are matching with your personal experiences.

Signs of a Gaslighter

Do you think you have a gaslighter around you? These are signs to look out for in their behaviors. Anytime you connect with an individual and begin to see these signs in them, try to cut off the connection as soon as possible. However, note that just a single sign the first time does not make it gaslighting, but one sign on multiple occasions or many signs at the first instance is a sure warning that the individual is a gaslighter.

1. Their words do not match their actions

Have you ever heard of the saying, "actions speak louder than words"?

When relating to gaslighting, following this saying's perspective is one of the most beneficial things you can do. If you ever feel victimized or trying to work out if you're being abused, always try to take note of what they are doing rather than what they are saying. For abusive people, what they say really means nothing; it's just talking.

What matters is focusing on what the person is actually *doing,* and this is where you'll find the issue. It has become a regular thing for their words to not line up with their actions; this is often one of the first signs you notice in their behavior as it's vital for gaslighting efforts to be effective.

When you see this sign in an individual at first, do not rush into making conclusions that someone is gaslighting you. As we spoke about already, one-off events happen from time to time, but it takes a consistent occurrence to make your suspicion valid.

In cases where there are mismatches between the actions and words of what someone is presenting you, allow your logical mind to go to work and start to question you. Which should you go for, the words or the actions?

For example, the person may be telling you things that are inspiring and strengthening but doing something different from that to you. Allow me to share an example of this. For instance, you are told how much you are cared for and appreciated, only for you to receive a comment that emotionally tears you apart. This is gaslighting when it happens consistently. Maybe you hear words about how you are loved and so unique, but you're being treated as a slave or someone with no value or significance.

Unfortunately, the natural gaslighting pattern and journey suggest that you'll probably find yourself always making excuses for them with thoughts like *He is perhaps stressed at the moment,* or *He appears to be in a bad mood,* etc. This consistent mismatch is not a mistake or coincidence; it is instead deliberate!

2. They tell blatant lies

Just like they are intentional with mismatched words and actions, so are they when it comes to lying and manipulating the truth. Whenever someone is talking to you, you know it is an outright lie if you are keen enough. Humans have a funny way of knowing whether someone is lying or not, and if you know something to be a fact and someone is lying directly to your face, what more proof do you need?

There are plenty of human behaviors that can help you identify when someone is lying that don't apply here. For example, if someone is lying and they know it, they will find it hard to make eye contact, unlike abusers who will feed you with lies with a straight face. For them, lies are not a bad thing; they are just another necessary means to an end. Thus, they tell you lies with a straight face with no form of guilt attached to it, which can make it hard to detect unless you're paying attention.

As much as they are not afraid or ashamed to tell you these lies in the open, they are also bold to even say that you do not need proof to reveal it is a lie, straight to your face. And you wonder, why are they so blatant? Is this person serious? Is she telling me all of these and expecting me to believe her? If you've felt this way but then allowed yourself to be treated with disrespect by being lied to consistently, you're being gaslighted.

Do not doubt it: abusers know what they are doing. And if you are not cautious enough, before you know it, you'll become trapped. Blatant lies are deliberate for gaslighters because they are setting up a precedent. Once they tell you a huge lie, you are not sure if anything they say is real. But more importantly, from that moment on, you are no longer sure whether anything else they say is true or false. Keeping you unsteady with an environment of doubt in your mind is the goal.

Couple this with everything we've spoken about in the previous chapter, such as doubting your own self-worth and having a lack of confidence in yourself. These lies are the cherry on the cake.

3. They deny they ever said/promised something

Let's say an abuser told you they would do something; you know you heard it, and you may even have the proof to show for it. Do they keep to their word, or does the abuser wholly deny it? This can happen in many ways, whether it's saying they'll go shopping or meet your family on a particular day, stating they'll stop taking drugs or having an affair, or recalling a past experience.

However, since they did not keep their word, you expect them to give you an apology or make an excuse, but no, they don't because they never said they would. This is another way in which you'll start questioning your reality. *Did he say that? Did she make such a promise? Is my proof valid? Maybe he said it but meant something else? Did I misinterpret what was said?*

Do you notice you start getting confused in these kinds of situations? You might tell yourself that you need to learn the other person's communication style as you are just recently connecting with them and still getting to know them, so you let it fly. You may think this will help you understand them better instead of making assumptions about what they actually mean. Hopefully, this will help make peace and reduce friction between the two of you, and a beautiful, fruitful relationship can come of it.

This way of thinking is very logical and practical, and in many cases, it could be exactly what your relationship needs to blossom. However, with an abuser, this is nothing to write home about as it will never work. As you allow the lies and manipulation of the truth to spread and become more commonplace, you increasingly doubt your reality and begin to accept theirs since you know no difference. This is how you become trapped in their web.

4. They project their evils/dark side onto you

Let's say that your partner is cheating on you, just as an example. It could be any kind of negative or abusive behavior, such as drinking, drug-taking, taking trips without telling you, gambling, and so on. As a cheater, you will find the abuser will start accusing you of cheating. Since they are blatant liars and manipulate the truth to suit the reality they want to create, they, in their stead, accuse you of being the liar, projecting their behavioral characteristics that are unacceptable all onto you. You are saying that she has promised to do something, but she claims she never said it, and if you insist, she could accuse you of trying to manipulate her into doing something you want. See how the abuser will flip the tables?

I remember in an earlier relationship of mine when my boyfriend (I must have been around 20 to 22) was convinced I was cheating. He would continuously try looking over my shoulder to see who I was texting, check my call log, etc. He would endlessly get paranoid about who I was seeing, or if I went to get drinks with friends after work, he would always be checking up to see what I was doing. It was a crazy amount of control and completely overwhelming. And guess what? He was cheating the entire time by still seeing and sleeping with his ex-girlfriend. I hadn't even so much as looked at another guy.

If the gaslighting abuse occurs in a romantic relationship setting, you'll see signs of this happening. They may suddenly "realize" that you do not even love them. You are only using them for your selfish interests. Don't worry. They're going to tell you this over and over again, seemingly out of nowhere, when insecurity strikes. If you're experiencing abuse in the workplace, the victimizer suddenly discovers that you never do any work. You are only getting paid for doing nothing. These are claims they'll make to both you and other people around, but only when it suits them.

As we spoke about above, remember that actions speak louder than words. If someone suddenly exclaims, you're not pulling your weight and not doing any work, this will tend to be a dramatic projection of the self, meaning that they are probably not doing much work, and they're attempting to shift the blame. Try not to take their words to heart, but instead focus on the reality of the situation and what is happening.

However, when this kind of projection is done so frequently, and if you're listening to their words and not focusing on reality, you'll find yourself beginning to defend yourself and are, therefore, distracted from the gaslighter's actual behavior. And so the snowball starts to roll.

5. They make use of what is near and dear to you as ammunition

Personal attacks are the bread and butter of gaslighting abuse because it takes what matters to you and uses it against you. Whether you're physically, spiritually, or emotionally bound to something or someone, this is a weak point since it's a topic where you may not be thinking straight. Therefore, it can be manipulated.

Many gaslighters would have gathered some foundational things about you like running background checks, family, kids, weaknesses, etc., near the beginning of a relationship. They may look through your social media profiles in detail, check your phone without you knowing, or in extreme cases, even bug or steal the passwords to your online accounts. While researching and writing this book, I spoke to a woman who picked up her date, perhaps on the third or fourth date, and had a lovely time. She took her car to the service garage a week later, only to find her date had placed a GPS location tracker under the wheel rim.

After gathering enough information about you, usually without your knowledge, the perpetrator will publicly speak against something very dear to you. This could be something that defines your personality, forms your identity. Thus, when used against you, the core of your being or existence has been attacked.

This is inhumane and wicked, but the gaslighter won't be affected in the way a typical person would. They have no remorse or guilt for their actions. They do not care and only care about how they would gain control, and this only comes to play when you get to depend on someone else and see them as the dearest fellow to you.

For instance, they might say something along the lines of, "The kids you have are not the right thing for you; you should not have had them. You would be far better off doing XYZ." They will also tell you, "You would be a worthy person if only you did not have a long list of negative traits." They attack the foundation of your being, who you are at your very core, and will go to great lengths in their attempt to degrade you.

6. They throw in positive reinforcement to throw you off

While gaslighting involves many negative attacks, passive-aggressive comments, and manipulation, things can get increasingly confusing since positive reinforcement is also a commonplace technique. Positive reinforcement, or saying things like "good job," "well done," and overall validating your behaviors or actions, is mostly used to teach or inculcate new behaviors.

Most times, positive reinforcement is used with children. If the child does something right, they get a reward or are told they are doing well. Over time, this stops the child from doing bad things and will make them more inclined to do good things. However, these techniques can also apply to teens and adults, and the outcome of the process depends on who's giving positive reinforcement.

This is very similar to how peer pressure works. When I went through a bit of a party stage during my early twenties, I experienced narcotic culture for the first time. Some of the older kids were hardcore cocaine users and would cheer and clap whenever one of their friends consumed more drugs than they usually would, claiming "the night is about to get crazy." This is a typical positive reinforcement, but being used in a harmful way. While the dangers of drugs and cocaine are well-documented and well-known, being cheered and edged on by people you care about makes it seem like you're doing a positive thing, and it makes you want to do it again.

Now, look at this from a gaslighting perspective. On the one hand, you have someone degraded you, attacking your core foundations, and bringing you down using words and actions. However, since this is someone you care about or are at least becoming reliant on when you do something that they want you to do, their positive words shine, which makes you light up and feel good about yourself. This makes you want to do whatever you're doing again, thus attracting more positive reinforcement. Ultimately, you become reliant on the abuser for your positive reinforcement, putting them firmly in control. It's an incredibly malicious process.

This becomes even worse when you're being degraded over and over again, far more often than you're receiving positive feedback. This lowers the bar to what you'll do to receive that positive validation. For example, tidying the house and cooking dinner was enough to make your partner happy and gave you validation. However, over time, this becomes not enough, and now you find yourself needing to get your partner's sexual attention, even when you don't want to, just to make them validate you. This is not a healthy place to be.

All of this comes together as a carefully planned attempt to keep you uneven and question your reality. As a rule of thumb, take a good look at what you were praised for and where you're getting validation in your relationships, and you'll find it probably benefits the gaslighter.

They recognize one thing that they love that you have done, rewards you (probably with a treat, words of affirmation, a gift, and the likes), making you feel good. As they build up your identity, you get stronger and empowered by their rewards. However, you must realize that they gradually destroyed your identity in the first place and are now building in you a new identity they want you to have. Are you aware that a deviation from whatever they want from you will make them flare up and tear you down again? That is, they have gained control over you and can choose to create and pull apart as they desire.

As a comparison, I've been off the road without a car for several years since I was living in a city and had no need for one, yet I've still always been an anxious driver. Upon moving out of the city, I decided it might be time to get back on the road again, and my partner fully supported me. It was nothing to do with him, just something I wanted to do for myself, yet the positive reinforcement was still there for following my dreams and desires.

7. They attempt to place people against you

Gaslighters are experts at exploiting you and other people around you that will stand by them and further their manipulated reality. Of course, it's going to feel incredibly isolating if there are people around you who are all agreeing that you should act and be a certain way. On the same premise as peer pressure, an abuser will gather people to their perspective in a bid to cement the abuser's gains and ensure they remain in control.

This can happen in many different ways, such as making you doubt the help of close friends and relatives by making comments such as, "Betty (your best friend) even knows that you are not right," or "Your mom knows you are useless and not worth good things too."

Keep in mind that just because an abuser is saying these things, it doesn't mean that these people actually said them. Remember, gaslighters are constant liars, so their words are almost entirely false or a misinterpretation of what has been said. When the gaslighter uses this tactic, you believe them, and you feel like you do not know who to trust or turn to. And of course, isn't it better to stay with the devil you already know? And that automatically leads you right back to the same person who gaslights you. This is precisely what they desire. With you becoming more isolated, you unconsciously put them further in charge and hand them more control.

What's more, the abuser will have already called you a liar by saying that you aren't telling the truth and things aren't as you remembered them. On top of this, they will tell you that everyone else (your family, friends, media, colleagues) are also liars, again making you question your reality. The chances are you've never known somebody with such a boldness to do this, so indeed what they must be saying is true? In reality, such outrageous claims sound so ridiculous that they simply couldn't be made up? No. They are. It's a control strategy. It makes victims go to the gaslighter for the "right" information, as you have come to take their words for the truth.

Within this bid to get people onto an abuser's side and practically against you, they begin telling people you are crazy. This is one of the most effective gaslighter tools to put you in isolation since it's contemptuous. It's hard to deny. Of course, a crazy person is going to say they're not crazy. How can you prove it either way? The fact is that typical people won't spout off such bold claims, which, strangely enough, gives the statements some credibility. The gaslighter understands that individuals will not doubt the abuser since they perceive them as abusive or out-of-control if people around you decide to question your mental soundness.

However, remember that the abuser can say to you that so-and-so thinks you're crazy or mad, when in fact, they haven't actually spoken to them whatsoever. It could just be another lie. On the other hand, if they have talked to people in your life to try and turn them against you, then it will take time, but you'll be able to speak up with people you can trust, but we'll get more into this throughout the following chapters.

Gaslighting is a subtle but cruel manipulation tactic that leaves the victims devastated and so torn apart. Keep the above signs in mind as you relate and connect with people to quickly look for a way to disconnect if you happen to ascertain a gaslighter around you. Again, this can feel like a lot to take in, and you might be feeling a little overwhelmed with all the information here, but that's okay.

Here's a takeaway section you can quickly refer to at any time.

Takeaways

In this chapter, we discussed some signs that you would personally see in you, indicating you are a victim of gaslighting. They are:

1. You lack joy and happiness in life
2. You pay attention to your character flaws
3. Your confidence is at a near-zero level
4. You always second-guess yourself and feel befuddled
5. Decisions are quite hard for you to make
6. Making apologies is what you do now and then
7. You have the feeling of being a failure
8. You feel detached from the individual you were used to
9. You lie to yourself as well as other people to dodge confrontations
10. You rationalize the conduct of the gaslighter and are tensed up around them
11. You are wondering if you are excessively sensitive in any case
12. You sense something is not right, yet you can't figure out what
13. You are withholding information from others

We also discussed some warning signs you will see in an individual that would indicate they are gaslighters. These signs would help you steer clear of these individuals as soon as you are sure of this manipulative act in them.

1. Their words do not match their actions
2. They tell blatant lies
3. They deny they ever said/promised something

4. They project their evil onto you

5. They make use of what is near and dear to you as ammunition

6. They throw in positive reinforcement to throw you off

7. They try to align people against you

Quick Checklist

From the takeaways above, can you mark some personal signs that you are already experiencing that showcase you are a victim of gaslighting?

_____

_____

_____

_____

_____

_____

Use this space to list some warning signs you see in an individual you have already earmarked as a gaslighter.

_____

_____

_____

_____

_____

_____

_____

Reflect on what you have written down.

Are the personal signs you are experiencing genuinely coming from this person, and are the warning signs consistent? This will help you take the necessary steps as quickly as possible to identify these signs early.

In the next chapter, we will be discussing gaslighting as a weapon, the phases involved in gaslighting, common gaslighting techniques, and its effects on health, relationships, social life, and work.

Chapter Three

Gaslighting, the Ultimate Weapon

"The weapon of choice for a narcissist is to make you feel as much guilt and shame as possible. You end up with the conviction that everything happening is your fault, that you are the crazy person they have made others believe you are. You are not crazy; you are being gaslighted."-K. Masters

Regardless of whichever way you choose to look at it, gaslighting is a brutal act. This act aims to degrade the mind of someone in such a way that the person becomes susceptible to the control or suggestion of another person. I choose to describe this act as a weapon because it's so damaging to a person's psychology and emotions. It is a weapon used to violate the love and respect of the victim.

Throughout the following sections of this chapter, I will take the time to explore the different phases of gaslighting and how each phase builds and snowballs the damage. This can help you to identify where you are, how the malicious act works, and ultimately how to get what kind of help.

The Phases Involved in Gaslighting

De Canonville (2020) stated that gaslighting happens in phases, not all at once. It takes time to build up the trust and the needed validation of the victim to work. While debated and subjective, there are typically three stages involved in gaslighting:

- The Idealization Phase

- The Devaluation Phase
- The Discard Phase

Understanding each phase and what it contains, a victim can (especially in the early phases) realize that they are being gaslighted. Then they can safeguard or defend themselves by walking away (physically or metaphorically). Let's take a moment to explore each in detail.

Phase One – Idealization

In this phase, also known as the "initial phase," the narcissist (or gaslighter) wears a seemingly good look to shape their victims into a symbiotic relationship with them. They come across as charming, attractive, and someone you'd want to spend time with, hence encouraging you to want to form a relationship with them.

Right from the very onset of the relationship, the narcissist pours a ton of attention onto their victim; that is, they are loving, charming, flirtatious, energetic, exciting, and significantly enjoyable to be around. They appear to be so glad and keen in the relationship by all accounts, and the clueless victim appreciates each second with their new magnetic accomplice. And who can blame them? If you're showered with affection and made to feel like the most important person on the planet, then of course you're going to want to be around that person.

The victim loves how the narcissist is so beautifully intense and how they seem to get drunk on life; hence, the victim wants to be a part of this bubble. Intense bonding begins for the victim right from the offset, who innocently believes that the narcissist feels the same way about them. The relationship is reciprocal; however, this is the narcissist's biggest deception, and the first step that has been taken.

Engrossed in this alluring state of excitement, the victim becomes hooked by the abuser's enthusiasm and impressive exaggerations. On a scientifically physical level, the victim is physically changing as though a typical relationship is being formed. Strong neural links form relating to this new person. Victims are known to experience biochemical and structural changes in the body and brain, respectively, in this relationship. These exciting hooks create a release of chemicals, called endorphins, in the brain.

These endorphins (commonly referred to as "pleasure substances") make the victim feel euphoria during this first phase of the relationship. Like addicts who respond to their habitual impulsive ways because of the same chemicals, victims become highly addicted and not so soon find themselves hooked emotionally to their narcissistic suitor.

However, this honeymoon phase is only an illusion. Smoke and mirrors. Having determined the victim's strengths and weaknesses expertly, the idealization phase is over, and it is time for the devaluation phase of the gaslighting to begin. Henceforth, the narcissist seems to turn cold, unfeeling, and even bitingly cruel.

Phase Two – Devaluation

As the relationship shifts from phase one to phase two, the abuser begins to behave as if a lethal freak fog has descended over life. Whereas before the abuser was high on life, thought everything was beautiful, and was very attractive and exciting to be around, this has changed in seemingly an instant, and for no plausible reason whatsoever. All of a sudden, the narcissist has become decisively cold and uncaring. The victim cannot seem to do anything right anymore; their fall from grace is hard. The narcissist's once sweet words turn to hard-hitting, deeply cutting criticism.

Everything the victim attempts ends negatively, thereby finding him or herself devalued at every turn. Confused by the narcissist's strange behavior, the victim has no clue what is going on. They become progressively focused, sad, and discouraged with the circumstance, leaving them in constant disorderliness.

The victim then works increasingly hard to satisfy their victimizer with expectations of getting the relationship back to where it was initially when they had a sense of security, and everything seemed bright and beautiful. However, despite the victim's hard work, they are suddenly thrown into intense withdrawal symptoms—distraught with anxiety, turned inside out with confusion, and stripped of what they thought they had: a soul mate.

In dealing with the pain of neglect and rejection, the victim adopts a series of oblivious guard systems (a blend of infantile regressive patterns, justification, trauma bonding, denial, cognitive dissonance, and the likes) as the only means of survival. By being involved in these survival strategies, the victim turns into the prisoner to the abuser, and in many ways to themselves and their own way of thinking, excessively reliant on their hostage taker (Stockholm syndrome), where the order for the day is unpredictability and uncertainty.

They relapse into infantile regressive patterns of conduct, known as regressed infantilism. This is basically a process in the mind, in human psychology, where someone is subject to trauma so intense that the mind does everything it can to block it out and make it seem as though nothing is happening. As a child would when scared, they look to the closest person, usually the child's mother, and will act helpless and dependent on that individual. This is a very natural survival strategy.

However, when it comes to the world of gaslighting, a similar process occurs. Since the victim is so degraded by the abuser, especially after going through such a subjectively perfect time during the first phase, this is an act of trauma on the brain, even at a biological level.

Just like a child, the victim will lose their maturity, will become unable to help themselves, and will become dependent on the person closest to them, which is usually the abuser themselves. It's a human survival technique gone mad. What's more, the victim is usually completely unconscious of this process happening.

The more the casualty shows their pain, the more they become a narcissistic supply for the victimizer, and the more significant and extraordinary the abuser gets the opportunity to feel when it comes to control and power. The more substantial and incredible the victimizer feels, the more glaring their verbal and physical viciousness becomes.

This "pull-push" situation leaves the narcissist acting in such a way that says, "I disdain you, yet don't you dare leave me, or I will execute you." They will respond to any apparent development away from them as a danger to their narcissistic supply, meaning it's time to turn the dial the other way and pull the victim back in. Accordingly, any demonstration of self-determination by the victim will unquestionably be degraded.

The narcissist is heartless in the manner they debase the person in question. The victim's devaluation can be conveyed through various structures and assaults (such as the victim's own attachment needs, intellectual capabilities, physical body and appearance, sexuality, creativity, etc.). By this time, the victim has been conditioned and cannot escape from that narcissistic individual. The victim is at a heightened risk of future re-exploitation and captures with other narcissists since they are prepared, such that different narcissists can spot them easily, almost as though it's on impulse.

Phase Three - Discarding

Discarding is the final phase, and in my opinion, one of the worst. With what started as the victim's idealization over the narcissist, it's nearly always destined to end with the romanticizing of the narcissist by the victim's over-dependence. In this final phase, the narcissist is indifferent to any needs or demands that the victim may have such that they no longer exist in their mind. In contrast, they are left confused for the victim and are eager to find solutions to fix the withering relationship, perhaps even unsure why things have turned out the way they have.

The person the victim used to be is no longer the same person, but has instead been replaced by an immature, dependent, isolated version of that. Be that as it may, the narcissist opposes all endeavors to protect the relationship, and the victim becomes worthless to them. The abuser wants the relationship to end because there is no longer any satisfaction to be had in it. Any attempt to win them back by the victim will only take care of the narcissist's inner self and further give them a transient wellspring of narcissistic supply.

Now, that doesn't mean that the relationship will end straight away. The needs of the abuser will come and go, and the push and pull effect will continue for a potentially long time. Sometimes months, years, or maybe even decades. Some victims will never escape their abusers.

Within these phases, the abusers will use a variety of gaslighting techniques, most of which we'll be exploring throughout the next section.

Common Gaslighting Techniques

Gaslighting techniques hide truths that the abuser doesn't want the victim to realize and are used to create a false reality. Hence, these techniques make gaslighting challenging to identify. However, with a bit of awareness and education about what you're looking for, they become easier to spot and understand. Some of the more common gaslighting techniques include (GoodTherapy, 2018; Tracy, 2019):

1. Withholding

This is a technique where the abuser refuses to listen to any concerns, pretends to lack understanding, and declines to share their emotions.

Examples:

    a) I don't have time to hear this nonsense.

    b) You're just trying to confuse me.

2. Countering

This is a technique where the abuser questions the victim's memory (experiences, thoughts, and opinions). An abuser may deny the events that occurred in the exact way the victim accurately remembers and invent details of the events that did not happen.

Examples:

    a) I heard you say it! You never remember our conversations right.

    b) You imagined that last time, and you were wrong.

3. Forgetting/Denial

In this technique, the abuser pretends to forget events that have happened to disprove the victim's memory further. An abuser may also deny making promises that are important to the victim to avoid responsibility.

Examples:

   a) What are you talking about?

   b) I never promised you that.

   c) You are making that up.

4. Blocking/Diversion

The abuser employs changing the subject of a conversation to divert the victim's attention in this technique and may even twist a conversation into an argument about its credibility.

Examples:

   a) Have you been communicating with your sister again? She's always sticking stupid ideas into your head.

   b) You are hurting me on purpose.

5. Trivializing

This is affirming that a person is overreacting to hurtful behavior and can condition a victim to believe their emotions, needs, or thoughts are not valid, significant, or excessive.

Examples:

   a) You're so sensitive!

   b) Everyone else thought my joke was funny.

   c) Are you going to allow something like that to come between us?

Effects of Gaslighting

Now, we've spoken a lot about gaslighting and what it does emotionally and physically, but when it comes to actually recovering from gaslighting experiences, it's important to know exactly what you're dealing with and what kind of toll this psychological process is having on you.

And believe me, it's not just being trapped in a relationship that isn't very nice to be in.

1. Effects on Psychological Health

Perhaps most importantly, gaslighting can have a catastrophic impact on a person's psychological health. Being told that your behavior is dramatic, unimaginable, or over-emotional can lead to gaslighting, as it can gradually make you start to question your behavior and ideas. This is extremely dangerous; the way you view yourself powerfully influences everything when it comes to how you behave in your day-to-day life (Shipp, 2020).

This kind of abuse affects how you engage with the people around you and how you go about setting and chasing goals. Suppose you are perpetually unsure of yourself, riddled with doubt and anxiety, and wholly dependent on the person who is gaslighting you. In that case, you are vulnerable to developing severe anxiety, depression, and other mental health concerns that can pose serious health risks. Hence, a pathway to effectively losing your sense of agency—that is, gaslighting is often gradual, chipping away or damaging the person's self-confidence and self-esteem, trust in themselves, reality, and the openness to love again (De Canonville, 2020).

Post-traumatic stress and codependency are also common developments. Some survivors may struggle to trust others, and they may be on consistent guard for further manipulation. This can take years to fully move on from. The person may blame themselves for having no prior awareness of the gaslighting act, again shattering their confidence in themselves, and their self-esteem since they're left asking, "Why was it me that fell for this?" or "How can I not be strong enough to look after myself?"

I can assure you right here and now that you are strong enough to look after yourself. You just found yourself falling victim to a deeply manipulative psychological process carried out and conducted on people by narcissists.

However, this refusal to show and share weaknesses can cause strain in future interactions. Some other survivors may get edgy for approval. They may attempt to keep others around them with satisfying human practices while ignoring any shame and guilt they may be feeling. Dangerously, this kind of accommodation may put them in danger of being another abuser's target.

2. Effects on Relationships

Of course, gaslighting massively affects most relationships while the abuse occurs, not just with the abuser, but also with people around the victim and their life.

When victims try to oppose a gaslighter, they often employ tactics to make them second-guess what they saw. The old saying, "I don't want you, but I don't want anyone else to have you," is an excellent illustration of how a gaslighter works. Their craving to have a person in their lives is more of a governing issue than love or a romantic affair. If, in the end, a victim leaves, an abuser has to find someone else to condition and grow the abuse from square one.

Gaslighting in relationships that are not intimate can happen too. Adult children may make their parents feel incapable of caring for themselves and that no one is available to offer them help to cause them to believe they should be admitted to a nursing home. The parent may be self-sufficient and still competent in self-care and provision.

Still, the adult child who is gaslighting may not want to be bothered and uses various methods to make them question their capability to remain self-sufficient. They may change things in the home to an entirely different place to make the parent uncertain and then act like the parent is absentminded. This may take place because the gaslighter does not want the eventual responsibility of caring for an aging parent or because he wants rulership of the parent's home or other possessions.

Even after a victim has managed to get out of an abusive relationship, no matter what type of relationship, the abuse can still affect future relationships. The victim may find it hard to be themselves or rediscover themselves and won't be ready to fully trust in new relationships out of fear of going through the same experience again.

However, the want and desire to have relationships with other people, which is a completely natural human impulse to have, can be messy because the victim still holds on to the mental barriers and defenses, meaning they can't fully commit themselves—their true selves—to the relationship, and this is at no fault of their own. It just takes time to become confident in your true self once more.

3. Effects on Social Life

Gaslighting will always affect a person's social life, and there are plenty of ways this can happen. The abuser may manipulate the victim into cutting ties with friends and family. The person might also isolate themselves, accepting they are shaky or unlovable. Even after the individual escapes the abusive relationship, the impacts of gaslighting can persist. The individual may even continue to question their observations and experience difficulty in decision-making due to what they have experienced. They are also less inclined to voice their feelings and emotions, realizing that they will probably be refuted (GoodTherapy, 2018), even if this isn't the case.

4. Effects on Work

According to Dean (2020), gaslighting can disrupt your work performance and harm your emotional and physical health, regardless of whether the gaslighting is happening at work itself or home. When there is someone at work who gaslights you, it can cause you to lose focus, and ultimately, you'll find yourself having difficulty performing your roles. The profound stress of being gaslighted can cause you to make errors you have never made before, or you may isolate further by avoiding required meetings, not returning calls or emails, and so on. For example, someone could gaslight you by reporting you for not doing your job correctly when you know you didn't make the written mistakes they're reporting you for.

Takeaways

Conclusively, one needs to be informed as to what gaslighting phases look like. In that way, the individual will be able to effectively understand and pinpoint what is occurring at these various phases, which are:

    i.   Idealization phase
   ii.   Devaluation phase
  iii.   Discarding phase

Also, there is a huge need for individuals to familiarize themselves with the common gaslighting techniques to enhance the identification of when one is being gaslighted. These techniques include:

i.   Withholding
ii. Countering
iii. Forgetting or denial
iv. Blocking or diverting
v.   Trivializing

More so, one will be able to spot if they are being gaslighted in any interpersonal relationships at home, socially, or otherwise, and guard themselves by keeping the narcissist out of their energy field, thereby, an escape route to gaslighting effects which are:

i.   Constant self-doubt
ii.   Low self-esteem
iii. Social isolation and withdrawal
iv.   Altered perception about reality
v.   No trust in own judgment
vi.   Psychological or mental trauma
vii. Stressed-out feelings
viii. Depression/Lack of self-confidence
ix.   Anxiety
x.   Decreased decision-making ability

These can have a drawn-out effect on somebody's emotional well-being and confidence. They may likewise make it more difficult for the person to leave an abusive environment.

Remember, gaslighting can happen in its own way, and while you may not have some feelings or experiences, you may have others. The most important thing to remember when it comes to identifying phases and signs is consistency. Sure, someone might make you feel anxious or say you're being silly once or twice over a long period of time. If it's happening all the time, then this is something that should concern you.

Quick Checklist

i. Take a moment to carry out a quick check on the gaslighting relationships you are in, list these relationships, and highlight which phase of gaslighting you are in.

_____

_____

_____

_____

_____

_____

If you happen to be in the early stages, then congratulations! Walking away physically or metaphorically is advised. Of course, this may be easier said than done, but with the support of your friends and family, perhaps a professional therapist or counselor, and open communication, you'll be able to get through it.

However, if you happen to be in the latter stages, I will also say congratulations. Do not lose hope; you are already on the path to successfully recovering from the vicious act.

ii. Take a rundown on the listed gaslighting effects in the takeaways above. Which of these are you already experiencing? Write down how they are affecting your health, social life, relationships, and work.

_____

_____

_____

_____

_____

Once you've done this, you should start to have a clear idea of how gaslighting affects your life in all the different aspects, giving you a greater understanding of yourself, your situation, and where your road to recovery begins. I've mentioned a little bit about narcissism, but if you're unsure what it is entirely, then this next chapter is for you.

Following on from phases and tactics, we're going to be going deep into the foundations of gaslighting, where we'll be discussing narcissism, what Narcissistic Personality Disorder (NPD) is, their traits, and so on, as they are the major ones who employ the use of gaslighting on their victims.

Chapter Four

What Is Narcissism?

"Half the hurt done in this world is owing to people who want to feel more important...They justify it because they are engrossed in the endless struggle to think well of themselves." - T.S. Elliot

Narcissists are involved in a wide range of behaviors that produces uncertainty, isolation, and even feelings of distrust in the memories of their partners. These are done through many acts, one of which is gaslighting. Narcissists are the majority of people who employ this form of verbal and psychological abuse to control and manipulate their victims.

Therefore, while you can get narcissists in all walks of life (many believe you have to be a narcissist at least a little to even be a celebrity), we'll dedicate this chapter to taking a look at what narcissism is, its traits, what and when it is considered a personality disorder, misconceptions about it, its types and faces, and other things to help you in achieving your recovery from this abuse.

The Definition of Narcissism

The term narcissism is often used to characterize a person with an increased sense of self-worth. It is also the pursuit of gratification from vanity or egotistic admiration of one's idealized self-image and attributes. It is portrayed by an inflated mental self-image and addiction to the imagination, by a surprising coolness and levelheadedness shaken only when the narcissistic boldness is undermined, and by the inclination to underestimate others or to abuse them. Narcissism is a distinct stage in children's development, yet it is viewed as a disorder when it happens after pubescence (Rhodewalt, 2020).

A narcissist is widely deployed to refer to people who appear too full of themselves. An individual who exhibits narcissistic traits may have a personality disorder known as Narcissistic Personality Disorder—NPD (Kritz, 2020). A personality disorder affects a person's thoughts, behaviors, and relationships with others. A personality disorder's essential features include impairments in personality (self and interpersonal) functioning and pathological personality traits.

In other words, people who are very selfish and only think of themselves are narcissists. Sure, we all have a bit of this within us, commonly referred to as "ego," because, of course, we want people to think about us in a good light. That's a basic human social instinct. However, it becomes a problem when this is all the person thinks about, and when they seriously damage others along the way.

While it involves looking better than anyone else, whether it's about looking good, or being seen doing good things, it can also be about putting others down in order to seem bigger than them and in front of those around them, which is the case with gaslighting.

When Is Narcissism a Personality Disorder?

Every human being will experience narcissistic properties in themselves from time to time. Nonetheless, those inclinations become a personality disorder when an individual's capacity to work and relate with others—that is, the relationship—is affected. People who are narcissistic show extreme confidence, crave attention, and show little empathy for others publicly. I'm sure you can start to see now why many celebrities are referred to as being a narcissist.

However, underneath this outward appearance of boldness, they regularly experience the ill effects of weak confidence that requires this desire for consistent approval, accompanied by sentiments of misery or insufficiency and an inability to create lasting relationships (Kritz, 2020).

Additionally, extreme narcissism can cross over to a mental illness called Narcissistic Personality Disorder, and the clinical evaluation of narcissism is known as a narcissistic personality disorder. This is a continuous and pathological pattern and causes distress and dysfunction to a person.

What is Narcissistic Personality Disorder (NPD)?

Narcissistic Personality Disorder (NPD) refers to a mental state characterized by an individual's undesirable view of themselves as being better than and more important than the individuals around them. Individuals with a narcissistic personality disorder might be commonly troubled and disillusioned when they are not given the unique favors or deference. They also have an over-inflated sense of dominance, entitlement, and prestige (Mandal, 2019), all of which they'll force onto other people.

However, beneath this exterior lies a very fragile self-esteem, low self-worth, and a constant need for validation. People with NPD are usually very sensitive when it comes to criticism. They may respond to criticism with hatred or rage and endeavor to deprecate others. These responses are alluded to as narcissistic rage. Statistically, NPD occurs more in men than in women.

Narcissism Traits

Just like with gaslighting, there are some key traits and signs you can look for to tell if someone is narcissistic. Remember, nearly everybody will show some of these traits at some point in their lives. That's natural. However, if you see these traits in something frequently and consistently, you're probably dealing with a narcissist.

Someone diagnosed with NPD tends to exhibit certain traits or characteristics (Bain, 2019; Cleveland Clinic, 2020):

1. An over-inflated feeling of pretentiousness, feelings of prevalence, and desire to only relate with high-status individuals.

2. Frequent thoughts about being more successful, influential, savvy, cherished, or appealing than others.

3. Need for unnecessary profound respect or special treatment.

4. Willingness to exploit others to accomplish their objectives with no regrets due to a lack of empathy.

5. A perceived sense of entitlement.

6. Lack of comprehension and consideration for other people's feelings and needs.

7. Extremely jealous and ultrasensitive.

8. Arrogant or snobby behaviors and attitudes.

9. Not taking criticism well.

Myths and Misconceptions about Narcissism

Not all assumptions about narcissism are valid. The term has been thrown around quite a bit over the last few years and lots of rumors and television characters etc., have kind of warped the meaning.

Some common myths and misconceptions popularly believed about narcissism include:

1. Confidence and Arrogance Always Signal Narcissistic Personality Disorder

The narcissistic traits or characteristics (such as someone who has a lot of confidence, maybe exaggerated, arrogant, obnoxious, or self-absorbed) alone do not signal that a person has a narcissistic personality disorder. This is so because they are precise; instead, in diagnosing a person with a narcissistic personality disorder, at least five of the narcissistic traits must be met. Such traits must also be exhibited consistently over time. Additionally, the symptoms must cause significant impairment or distress in a person's life and relationships (Ellis, 2020).

2. Narcissism is High Self-Esteem

One can be narcissistic and not have high self-esteem. The main difference is that individuals high in self-esteem pay attention to relationships, while narcissists lack caring about relationships (Miller, 2018). In other words, a relationship is just a means to an end that allows them a secure place to get their validations.

3. Women Cannot be Narcissists

It's a dangerous myth to assume women are not narcissistic, though more men are diagnosed with narcissistic personality disorder than women. More so, statistics indicate that about 75 percent of diagnosed cases are in men; hence, this fact means that 25 percent of patients are women (Ellis, 2020).

4. You Can Change a Narcissist

This is another harmful myth. It is not wrong to believe a narcissist can change, but it is false and damaging to think that one can change them on one's accord. One who tries to change someone with NPD is bound to be disappointed and hurt at worst (Miller, 2018; Ellis, 2020). Many believe it cannot be changed, or cured, but rather managed.

5. Narcissists Think of Themselves to a Very Great Degree

Individuals with NPD hide their feelings (such as self-doubt, low self-esteem, and often depression and anxiety) with an outward appearance of boldness and qualification. They see the negative feelings as a weakness that will make them look bad and lowers their value as a person. It is, therefore, noteworthy on the inside that they are struggling and often don't like themselves at all (Ellis, 2020).

6. Narcissism Can be a Healthy Personality Trait

As a personality trait and not as a clinical diagnosis in the aspect of narcissistic personality disorder (which is a spectrum), one may indeed relate to some parts of it that aren't bad in and of themselves (e.g., believing one is a good leader or seeing oneself as assertive). However, the more narcissistic a person is, the less healthy the trait is—especially for the people around them (Miller, 2018).

7. Narcissists Are Evil

It is understandable why some people may think this, especially after everything we've spoken about. The truth is that narcissists are people, flawed in their ways. They can mistreat people sometimes, but they are hurting on the inside and deserve empathy. All mental illnesses, of which NPD is one, are a struggle to live with, not just the ones that are outwardly obvious (Ellis, 2020).

8. Narcissistic Personality Disorder Isn't Treatable

Indeed, this is among the most difficult mental dysfunctions to treat; however, it isn't unthinkable. Nobody living with this condition, or adoring somebody with it, should lose hope. Experienced therapists can help individuals with NPD make positive progress over time (Ellis, 2020). As above, there's not so much a cure, but the condition can be managed over time.

Signs and Symptoms of Narcissism

People diagnosed with narcissism exhibit different signs and symptoms and varying severity levels. These signs include (Mandal, 2020; Kritz, 2020; Mayo Clinic, 2020):

1. An exaggerated sense of self-importance

2. Difficulty managing pressure and dealing with change

3. A sense of entitlement to special treatment

4. Feeling effortlessly insulted

5. Requiring and expecting excessive and constant admiration and praise

6. A reluctance or inability to perceive the feelings and requirements of others

7. A distraction with imaginations about magnificence, force, splendor, and achievement

8. Behaving in a presumptuous way that is seen as proud, egotistic, or vainglorious

9. Feeling discouraged if they do not meet up with their expectations (perfections)

10. An embellishment of talents and accomplishments

11. Envy of others

12. Difficulty in regulating one's feelings and behavior

13. An inclination to monopolize discussions

14. A demand for having the best, regarding property and position

15. Taking a bit of leeway of others

16. A conviction that other people are envious

17. Looking down on and belittling individuals

18. Feeling prevalent and looking for connections only with successful individuals of the same caliber.

19. Setting unrealistic goals

20. Becoming furious or restless if they do not get unique treatment

21. Secret feelings of shame, insecurity, vulnerability, and humiliation

22. Reacting with fury or disdain to cause oneself to appear to be unrivaled

23. Insist on having the best of everything (e.g., the best car, office, etc.)

Differences Between Being a Narcissist and Being Self-Centered

Now you may be thinking that you've probably met some self-centered and selfish people throughout your life. Are they narcissists? Sure, someone at work is a good leader and is able to get the job done, and they know they're good at it. Are they a narcissist? It's important to note that there is a difference between being a narcissist and a selfish person.

This is why in the introduction to this chapter, I said that the term narcissist has been warped over time. Various people often use the word narcissist loosely, but there are several subtle differences between being a narcissist and being just self-centered. Identifying the difference(s) can better enhance one's means of navigating one's relationship with those who seem self-involved (Wolff, 2018). They are:

A. Narcissists' Moods Depend on Others

The mood states of a narcissist are highly bound to who they are around, as well as the environment they're in. They need regulation from others to maintain their framework (self). On the other hand, a merely self-centered person won't have this weakening arrangement of clashing indications (e.g., outrageous reliance on others, while at the same time feeling prevalent and disdainful). A selfish person is just a selfish person all the time, no matter where they are or who they are with.

B. Narcissists Lack Empathy

A self-centered person is much more likely to understand the feelings of other people, unlike those with narcissistic personality disorder who have abnormalities associated with the brain that provides room for the feeling of empathy for others. Hence, people who have close relationships with them tend to experience hurts repeatedly. More so, this lack of ability of theirs to feel for others can have devastating impacts. This pattern will not be noticed in someone who is solely self-centered. A self-centered person will know when they have crossed a line and what they have done wrong, feeling guilt and remorse for their actions.

C. Narcissists Think They Are Better Than Others

Narcissists believe that they are smarter, more significant, and better than others. A self-centered person may crave attention and seek ways to bring others' attention to themselves, yet they are likewise capable of tuning in to other people when the time arises. They might not like someone else being in the spotlight, but they will allow it to happen. A self-centered person may desire to be noticed, but a narcissist feels a need to be seen and clear how they are superior to others.

D. Narcissists Are More Entitled

Narcissists can be absorbed in their belief that they deserve special treatment that others do not deserve. Self-centered people have more apparent moral values that can align with society and are guided by empathy and genuine care for others.

For example, a narcissist needs to be in control and feel as though they are on top. They may do this as the boss of a company by gaslighting their staff to feel in control. On the other hand, selfish people will just do things like fiddling the paperwork so another department can do the workload but do so with the rest of their own team in mind.

E. Narcissists Are Less Self-Aware

Self-centered people can have self-awareness such that if given the right feedback or opportunity for reflection, they can recognize how being self-centered could be problematic and actively work to make changes. In contrast, narcissists are not capable of this insight. Although narcissistic personality disorder can be managed with a therapist's aid, getting a narcissist to own up to a problem and see the therapist willingly is a challenge in itself.

F. The Relationships of Narcissists Are More Transactional

The relationships of narcissists are purely transactional. They need validation, assurance, and control, and the people they position in their lives provide this. Self-centered people still tend to have reciprocal relationships that are both give and take; they just might take more than they give. A narcissist tends to seek out partners and friends for their high status in some vital areas, such as being exceptionally beautiful, accomplished, socially prominent, well-to-do, or well-connected.

G. Narcissists Do Not Feel Guilty When They Wrong Others

True narcissists do not feel guilty or remorseful when they do something wrong, unlike people who are just self-centered (who also still have empathy). More so, they will never perceive themselves as being wrong; hence you can never expect a genuine apology from them.

H. Narcissists Are More Likely to Feign Interest

In addition to self-absorbed people, narcissists can glaze over when one tries to speak about anything apart from them, but a self-centered person is more likely to show an interest in what one is saying. This means that a self-absorbed person may genuinely want to be interested in what someone is saying but will have difficulty maintaining that interest. Generally, whether a narcissist feigns interest or switches topics depends on what they hope to gain from listening to one.

I. Narcissists Tend to Overreact

Narcissists are full of rage and vengeance whenever their perceived superior status feels threatened, and the result of the anger could be disastrous. More so, the punishment narcissists dish out will usually be way messed up with apparent regard to the perceived offense. Self-centered people might get bothered; however, their responses are not prone to be more outrageous than narcissists.

The Causes of Narcissism

The root cause of narcissism remains unclear. There is a likelihood of the disorder involving a combination of factors (Kritz, 2020; Mayo Clinic, 2020; Cleveland Clinic, 2020):

1. Environment: Mismatches in parent-child relationships with either unnecessary adoration or excessive criticism that is inadequately attuned to the child's experiences (such as physical, sexual, and verbal abuse)

2. Genetics - Inherited characteristics (e.g., family history)

3. Neurobiology - The interconnection between the brain and behavior and thinking (such as personality and temperament; hypersensitivity to textures, noise, or light in childhood)

Complications Associated with Narcissism

The complexities of narcissistic personality disorder and other conditions can occur alongside it (Mayo Clinic, 2020):

1. Relationship difficulties
2. Problems at work or school
3. Depression and anxiety
4. Physical health problems
5. Drug or alcohol misuse
6. Suicidal thoughts or behavior

How Is Narcissism Diagnosed?

There are no laboratory tests to diagnose narcissism. Its diagnosis is usually made based on several factors (Kritz, 2020):

1. A detailed psychological evaluation

2. A physical test to preclude any physical issues

3. An assessment of measures for diagnosis based on the most recent version of the Diagnostic and Statistical Manual of Mental Disorders (DSM-5), set and produced by the American Psychiatric Association

A diagnosis of NPD in the DSM-5 incorporates these criteria:

1. Issues with interpersonal relationships

2. Difficulty carrying on with life

3. Setting objectives depending on getting the endorsement of others

4. Seeking profound respect

5. Inability to relate in general

6. Inability to relate to the feelings of others

7. Having sentiments of entitlement

8. Trouble with intimacy

9. Standards that are unreasonably high and seeing yourself as unique

10. Being antagonistic

11. Excessive endeavors to attract and be the focal point of the attention of others

A diagnosis of narcissism necessitates that these personality traits proceed after some time, are predictable in various circumstances, are not typically dependent on the individual's stage of development, or their cultural or social environment. Most children and teenagers will have narcissistic tendencies as they grow up as a natural part of growing up, learning how to be, and finding themselves. It's also worth noting that narcissism is not the aftereffect of medication or alcohol use or prescription the individual is taking.

Prevention of Narcissism

Due to the unknown cause(s) of narcissistic personality disorder, prevention remains unknown (Mayo Clinic, 2020). However, it may help to:

- Get treatment early for early mental health problems. This involves parents becoming aware of the signs of narcissism and seeking help for their teenage children.

- Being involved in family therapy to know healthy ways of communicating or coping with conflicts or emotional distress.

- Attend parenting classes and seek guidance from therapists or social workers if necessary.

- Providing ample support to children who suffer abuse.

Treatment and Medication Options for Narcissism

Since there are no "cures" to narcissism, the condition must be managed as much as possible, but this becomes increasingly difficult the older someone is, and the more narcissist they are. As we've discussed, a narcissist doesn't want to admit there is a fault with them and will therefore be unlikely to actively want to seek help.

However, if dealing with a narcissist at a young age, or the individual is accepting of treatment, there are two main options they can use.

<u>Treatment</u>: NPD is treated with (Kritz, 2020):

1. Psychotherapy

2. Talk therapy

Psychotherapy can assist someone with NPD to interact with others more sympathetically and positively. Psychotherapy can likewise help individuals with NPD manage strong reactions and feelings that arise during the treatment and recovery process. Its effectiveness is relying on the severity of the condition.

Individual, couples, or group treatment can help individuals with NPD gain proficiency with a portion of these new emotional skills:

1. Understanding and controlling issues of self-confidence and accepting insecurities
2. Recognizing and tolerating what they should or shouldn't do, so it's simpler to deal with criticisms or disappointments
3. Understanding and controlling emotions
4. Accepting and keeping up close to home and work relationships
5. Not seeking objectives that aren't reachable

<u>Medications</u>: While medication is not explicitly given to treat narcissism, drugs may be prescribed for related symptoms such as anxiety or depression.

And with that, we come to the end of this chapter. Hopefully, it's been quite enlightening to hear all about narcissism and where it comes from. Even as a gaslighting victim, it's important to remember to treat the abuser with empathy. While gaslighting involves a lot of malicious practices, it really is not the fault of the abuser themselves, since they are in pain themselves and are simply reflecting how they feel on the inside and are trying to do the best they can with what they know.

Of course, many people are aware that there are other ways to live, and narcissists don't need to live and act the way they do. Opening them up to this way of thinking is a challenge in itself, but ultimately not your responsibility. Your responsibility lies with your own health and well-being, but hopefully, this chapter has opened your eyes to how being treated the way you have been is nothing personal but lies on the abuser and their condition.

Let's recap what we covered.

Takeaways

- Narcissism is simply the tendency to think very highly of oneself and to have little or no regard for others.
- Narcissism becomes a disorder known as Narcissistic Personality Disorder (NPD) when relationships with others are affected.
- A narcissistic personality disorder is an unhealthy feeling of self-importance over others. It is more frequently diagnosed in men than in women.
- Narcissism possesses various traits that make identification easy, such as an overinflated sense of importance, sense of entitlement, lack of empathy, etc.
- Myths and misconceptions also exist about narcissism based on people's assumptions, as the word has been thrown around over the last few years.
- Narcissism is shown via different signs in people of different ages, which occur at varying severity levels. These levels can also change over time.

- Narcissism can be recorded and diagnosed based on a scale of severity.

- Deciphering between a self-centered person and a true narcissist could pose difficult, but subtle differences help shed light on where they diverge.

- The leading cause(s) of narcissism is unknown; hence, its prevention remains unknown, and the condition cannot be corrected, but treatment can help.

- The treatment of narcissism occurs via psychotherapy and talk therapy.

- More so, there are no laboratory tests that can identify/diagnose narcissism; a mental health diagnosis is required.

- Medication can be prescribed to treat anxiety, depression, etc., that may accompany a diagnosis of NPD.

Quick Checklist

i. From the signs and symptoms listed above, is there anyone around you who seems to be a narcissist or suffering from NPD?

---

ii. Briefly, do a quick review of the subtle differences between a self-centered person and a narcissist. This is to verify if the person is a narcissist or just a self-centered person.

_____

_____

_____

_____

_____

In the next chapter, we will be discussing the various types of narcissists, what it can look like in different people, how severity affects narcissism, and what else to look out for.

Chapter Five

Types and Faces of Narcissism

"You might as well bang your head into a brick wall if you expect the narcissist to be reasonable, empathetic or human in any way. If you sense or witness any of these traits, there is an ulterior motive. When the narcissist is being nice, it is because they have something to gain." – Tina Swithin

Types of Narcissism

Generally, people seem to show a lot of interest in the concept of narcissism. Perhaps this interest is shown because human beings are naturally narcissistic in a few ways, or perhaps people know someone else who is narcissistic. With the rise and daily push of celebrity content thanks to media and social media, narcissism is, in essence, becoming fairly mainstream.

I won't name names, but many celebrities fit the bill perfectly. There are also lists online of celebrities who are supposedly narcissist, if you are interested. Regardless, many celebrities seem to think of themselves very highly, love the attention being on them, and won't respond well to criticism that makes them not seem as great in the eyes of the public. The access and reach of social media have also allowed anybody to have a chance at satisfying these supposed needs.

However, when it comes to tagging an individual in your own life as a narcissist, care needs to be taken because several narcissism types exist. Even though they all maintain the basic features of narcissism (entitlement, lack of empathy, and a need for control), they are revealed via different behaviors and vary in severity and danger.

Hence, knowing the different types of narcissism, their distinctive features, and safeguarding oneself when dealing with them is incredibly beneficial.

The idea of narcissism can be broken down into eight main groups. I'm also going to throw in some coping strategies at the end of each section, so if you're dealing with this kind of narcissist yourself, you have some actionable tips you can put into practice right away.

1. Healthy Narcissism

Every single person has a bit of healthy narcissism within them.

An individual with healthy narcissism will feel pride based on their accomplishments and willing to share them with others because it makes them feel good. Healthy narcissism is also the ability to perceive a sense of entitlement and knowing that one belongs in specific spaces and deserve good things (Moore, 2020). If the boss of a company or the captain of a sports team can step up and take responsibility when things are tough because they know they are a good leader, then this is beneficial to all.

2. Grandiose Narcissism

Grandiose narcissism is also referred to as exhibitionist narcissism. Grandiosity implies having an unrealistic sense of superiority or expertise. If you see someone who is a professional in something, and they talk as though they're the best and the only expert at what they do, this is an example of grandiose narcissism.

However, grandiose narcissism typically involves overestimating one's abilities, asserting one's dominance over others, and having a generally inflated sense of self-esteem. More so, when someone's narcissistic qualities (such as entitlement, powers, self-obsession, etc.) are displayed openly, it is usually at the detriment of others, such as saying, "I'm amazing, and this other person here isn't," thus trying to elevate themselves further and widening the gap of how good everyone is or isn't.

Grandiose narcissists can be attractive in some situations, especially if the people around are interested in the topic or subject, such as an adoring fan. Still, these narcissists usually lack empathy, and they don't relate well to other people in conversations and social interactions. This lack of kindness might be because they desire attention, enjoy seeing others hurt and confused, or both. They want to be on the center stage and are uncomfortable when they are not (Miller 2019; Moore, 2020).

For example, exhibitionist or grandiose narcissists have the "look at me" mindset children often have. Generally, children lack empathy when they are growing up because their parents will do everything for them and make them the center of their worlds. This is simply a lack of education since children don't know any better, nor understand how the world works. However, as the child grows up, and ensuring they receive a sufficient amount of attention, children learn empathy and grow out of their habits.

Yet, some people will develop and grow up in homes where the kids are *encouraged* to be narcissistic—for instance, they may be told their family name makes them unique and that they deserve success because it is "in your blood" (Dodgson, 2018).

Coping Strategies: Setting boundaries is necessary for dealing with a grandiose narcissist, so enforcing such limitations is essential. Boundaries could include having time to talk about you and things other than the narcissist, and spending time with others. Where needed, walking away could be a good alternative.

3. Vulnerable Narcissism

Covert narcissism, or closet narcissism, is also called vulnerable narcissism. Unlike grandiose narcissists, covert narcissists tend to be shy and self-effacing. This narcissism can be trickier to spot than other narcissism types because their disorder is not always blatant and sits off the curve on the narcissism scale and isn't typically how you'd expect a narcissist to be. Covert narcissists are reserved, manifestly distressed, and hypersensitive to the appraisals of others while chronically envious. They crave people's recognition and become very defensive in the face of criticism. Covert narcissists are frequently abjectly miserable and believe their suffering is worse than anyone else's (Miller, 2019; Moore, 2020).

For instance, a closet narcissist does not say, "I am special." Instead, they point to something else (a celebrity, a religion, a book, a dress designer, etc.), and say they are unique; hence, they feel special by association. A great example of this is when someone feels special because they're wearing a designer brand, and other people can tell and point it out. That is being special by association (Dodgson, 2018).

Coping Strategies: Truly, covert narcissists may have been hurt before, but one never has to rescue them or save them. This means boundaries must be put straight, and the narcissist could benefit greatly from talk therapy, where the hidden underlying issues or past trauma can be addressed and sorted through.

4. Malignant Narcissism

Malignant narcissists are also known as toxic narcissists. They are manipulative, malicious, and destructive, just as the name implies. This is the most severe type of narcissistic personality disorder because they show signs of sadism and aggression. They derive pleasure from seeing people writhe in pain and discomfort (for instance, abusing one physically, seeing to the loss of one's job, etc.). They have spent their lives perfecting the craft of becoming better narcissists (Miller, 2019; Moore, 2020).

Coping Strategies: Complete avoidance of a malignant narcissist and cutting off all ties is the best strategy. It's very rare that this kind of narcissist would ever feel the need to get help and will tend to bounce from one person to another, satisfying their needs for as long as they can.

5. Sexual Narcissism

These types of narcissists have an overly optimistic, egotistical admiration of their sexual prowess. They can become consumed by their obsession with sexual performance and the need for others' sexual respect. Sexual narcissists also often use sex to manipulate people and may behave violently during sex, usually starting out tame, but snowballing and becoming increasingly hardcore over time. They will usually seem to admire or fawn over someone, giving them everything they can, only to write one off once they have no use for them anymore (Miller, 2019; Moore, 2020).

Coping Strategies: The safest option to protect yourself from this narcissist type is to leave the relationship and seek therapy to help you get through the breakup with a narcissist. Since sex is such a physical, emotional, and biological activity, especially when it comes to connection, this can be one of the most destructive forms of narcissism.

6. Somatic Narcissism

Somatic narcissists deduce their self-worth from their bodies, and sometimes people who fall into this bracket will be seen as "peacocks." This form of narcissism may be apparent as someone feeling more beautiful, healthier, or fitter than others, as well as deriving a sense of superiority from it. Somatic narcissists usually obsess over their weight and physical appearance, and condemn others based on their appearance. Also, they typically ignore the needs of others and prioritize their own (Moore, 2020).

Coping Strategies: In dealing with a somatic narcissist, one needs to avoid displaying emotional responses to their peacocking behavior, recognizing it for what it is so you don't take their comments personally, and recognizing that they are putting you down to boost themselves up. Setting boundaries with what is and isn't acceptable to say to you is also essential.

7. Cerebral Narcissism

Cerebral narcissists are also called intellectual narcissists. They derive their self-importance from their minds and how intelligent they perceive themselves to be. Cerebral narcissists get their "hit" from feeling smarter, more creative, and more intelligent than others (Moore, 2020).

Coping Strategies: In dealing with a cerebral narcissist, one needs to insulate oneself from their words. It is necessary to note that a person is never going to win an argument or get to a point where they acknowledge that such a person is right; hence, it is better to learn to let it go.

8. Spiritual Narcissism

Spiritual narcissists often use their spirituality to justify harmful behaviors and use spiritual jargon to intimidate others. Spiritual narcissists use seemingly sensitive and spiritual actions as a way to elevate themselves above others. An individual who has experienced significant disruption (such as a divorce) is more prone to a spiritual narcissist's captivating and dynamic influence (Moore, 2020).

Coping Strategies: Isolating from a person who uses their spirituality to manipulate or belittle one is the best means of protection. Whenever the topic arises, recognize what is happening and detach from the situation without getting caught up in the details.

Faces of Narcissism

On top of narcissism types, there are typically two faces of narcissism (Hutson, 2015; Rogoza et al., 2018) you may come across; one being positive, and the other negative.

1. The Bright Face

This is also known as the "admiration-seeking face." The bright face reveals a high level of self-esteem. It is also characterized by extraversion and openness. Self-promotion, a feature of admiration seeking, draws praise. Admiration is positively linked with cognitive empathy, which results in social desirability.

A bright-faced narcissist will be positive, cheerful, and very attractive. Naturally, many people are drawn to this kind of narcissist because they portray themselves as the ideal kind of human, making the people around them question why they aren't like that.

2. The Dark Face

This is also referred to as the "rivalry face." The dark side of narcissism is predominantly related to low empathy, which underpins its unfriendly and socially exploitative character. Also, the dark face displays shyness and loneliness. Additionally, self-defense, which is a trait of rivalry, demeans others to fend off criticism.

Of course, a narcissist of any kind could wear either mask, or will use a combination of both, depending on the situation and the specific relationship. A bright face may be used during the initial stages of the relationship but will turn to the dark face once the narcissist is done using the person.

Narcissistic Abuse

It is noteworthy that abuse and narcissism are not always related. A diagnosis of narcissistic personality disorder does not automatically translate to abusive behavior, just like when many people who engage in abuse do not have a narcissistic personality disorder. More so, some narcissists' coping mechanisms themselves can be abusive, hence the term "narcissistic abuse" (Lancer, 2020).

Narcissistic abuse, according to Gulla (2020), is any domestic abuse (could be physical, financial, emotional, sexual, among others) that is carried out by somebody (the abuser or narcissist) with **narcissistic traits**. That is, their selfish behavior will negatively impact the way they behave towards a person (the abused) to manipulate, control, and instill a sense of worthlessness in the other person (the victim).

This includes gaslighting.

A narcissistic abuser could not necessarily be just an intimate partner but also a parent, family member, boss, colleague, or friend. People who are frequently abused by narcissists tend to believe a distorted version of reality as they are repeatedly lied to and manipulated. They tend to doubt everything and find it difficult to trust others as they have been modified to do so by their abuser (Myupchar, 2019).

Signs Associated with Narcissistic Abuse

The signs that indicate a person is experiencing narcissistic abuse to look for include (Raypole, 2020):

A. False Perfection - Narcissistic abuse tends to follow a clear or seemingly perfect pattern, though this pattern might vary slightly based on the type of relationship. If someone's life is coming across as being perfect, this can indicate a problem.

B. Doubt from Others - Narcissistic abuse is often hard to grasp such that when it occurs in public, it might become so well played out that others hear or see the same attitude and fail to recognize them as abuse. That is, doubting the occurrence even though it was noticed.

C. Smear Campaigns - People with narcissistic traits often need to maintain their perfect image to keep earning admiration from others by making someone else's look terrible. For instance, once a person begins pointing out problems or questioning the narcissist's behavior, they might respond by directing their rage toward the person openly with insults and threats or criticizing them, attempting to switch the focus of the conversation.

D. Isolation - Loneliness sets in when one lacks a listening ear from his or her loved ones, resulting in further manipulation. The abuser may also pull one back in with kindness, even apologizing if they have to, or pretending the abuse never occurred. This tactic is known as *hovering*, and it often works better when the victim lacks support.

E. Freezing - The natural response to abuse and other trauma differs. Usually, one may attempt confronting the abuser (fight) or escaping the situation (flight), but, in extreme cases where these methods fail or an inability lies in their usage, one might respond by freezing instead. The freeze response usually happens when one feels helpless, and it often involves dissociation.

F. Indecision - Narcissistic abuse often involves frequent implications that you have trouble making good decisions and doing things right. A model of devaluation and criticism can leave one with minimal self-esteem and confidence.

G. Self-Blame - A key feature of narcissism is difficulty blaming any negative deed or harmful behavior. Abusive partners typically find some means to cast blame on you. Forced by deceit, the victim will often insist that they could not recollect something said by them in the past, or the abuser may become so angry that it can result in pacifying the victim into apologizing, agreeing that they were in the wrong, not the abuser.

H. Physical Symptoms - Abuse can initiate anxious and nervous feelings that sometimes lead to physical symptoms such as appetite changes, nausea, abdominal pain or other gastrointestinal distress, muscle aches and pains, insomnia, fatigue, etc.

I. Restlessness - Narcissistic abuse can sometimes be unpredictable, and often is. That is, one may not know whether the victim will face criticism or get rewarded at any particular time. One may develop a lot of tension from needing to prepare oneself to face conflict and worries regularly may sometimes cause one not to feel relaxed anymore.

J. Loss of Self - Many people eventually adjust their self-identity to give an abusive partner allowance when facing abuse (e.g., one spends time doing what one's partner wants to do, in order to showcase that one does care). These changes usually lead to a loss of one's sense of self, leaving one with a feeling of emptiness, and can eventually lead to having a hard time enjoying life.

K. Boundary Issues - Setting healthy boundaries is essential to any relationship, detailing what can and can't be said and done; however, setting boundaries can pose difficulties for one experiencing narcissistic abuse. An abuser or narcissist usually has little respect for borders and boundaries, which could extend to one's relationships with others and may eventually lead to the victim giving up on their own boundaries entirely.

L. Anxiety and Depression – Anxiety and depression commonly grow as a result of narcissistic abuse. The primary stress you face can trigger persistent feelings of worry, nervousness, and fear. Also, one may even feel hopeless or worthless and lose interest in things that generally brings joy.

Recovering from Narcissistic Abuse

Abuse, no matter its kind, can take a significant toll on a person's emotional and physical health. Whether one is just starting to notice the early signs of narcissistic abuse or is trying to heal from previous experiences and trauma, therapy could help by providing opportunities to learn coping strategies through the following steps (Raypole, 2020b):

- Acknowledge and accept the abuse

- Set your boundaries and state them clearly

- Prepare for complex emotions

- Reclaim your identity

- Practice self-compassion

- Understand that your feelings may linger

- Take care of yourself

- Talk to others

- Get professional support

Takeaways

- There are different types of narcissism, and they include:

  a) Healthy narcissism

  b) Grandiose or exhibitionist narcissism

  c) Vulnerable/covert/closet narcissism

  d) Malignant or toxic narcissism

  e) Sexual or seducer narcissism

  f) Somatic narcissism

  g) Cerebral or intellectual narcissism

  h) Spiritual narcissism

- The best thing to do to guard oneself when dealing with someone suspected to have a narcissistic personality disorder or, better still, after identifying a person's type of narcissism, is to set healthy boundaries and ideally stay clear or walk away from the relationship altogether.

- There are two faces of narcissism:

  a) The bright or admiration-seeking face

  b) The dark or rivalry face

- It is important to observe that not all narcissists show the two faces of narcissism.

- The two faces of narcissism each have different effects on body language, relationship health, and personality.

- Narcissistic abuse is a kind of domestic abuse similar to more comprehensive emotional abuse and coercive control.

- The signs that a person is experiencing narcissistic abuse are:

    a) False perfection

    b) Doubt from others

    c) Smear campaigns

    d) Isolation

    e) Freezing

    f) Indecision

    g) Self-blame

    h) Physical symptoms

    i) Restlessness

    j) Loss of self

    k) Boundary issues

    l) Anxiety or depression

    m) Reaching out

- Therapy could proffer a healing process from narcissistic abuse.

Quick Checklist

A. As an individual, evaluate yourself to know the category of narcissism you belong to or exist in your relationships to understand the coping mechanisms. Then, write down the category of narcissism you are experiencing.

_____

_____

_____

_____

B. Hence, determine whether you fall into the admiration of the bright face or the dark face of narcissism.

C. Finally, figure out if you are experiencing narcissistic abuse based on several signs observed, write down these signs of narcissistic abuse, and if you are, seek to apply the recovery tips.

_____

_____

_____

_____

_____

This checklist helps you set healthy boundaries and ideally stay clear or walk away from the relationship altogether if you are suffering from narcissistic abuse.

Chapter Six

Emotional and Psychological Abuse

"An abused can seem emotionally needy. You can get caught in a trap of catering to him, trying to fill a bottomless pit. But he's not so much needy as entitled, so no matter how much you give him, it will never be enough. He will just keep coming up with more demands because he believes his needs are your responsibility until you feel drained down to nothing." -Lundy Bancroft

Abuse

Simply put, abuse is abuse, no matter the diagnosis of the abuser. As we've spoken about already, an abuser is a troubled and tortured individual, and like all human beings in any situation, you should always aim to provide them with empathy.

Yes, there is no excuse for being abused, but having been through it, I feel very sorry for my ex-partner because he was living in so much pain. To have the insecurities and the constant need for validation that he had can't be a pleasant life to live. However, that doesn't mean you should put up with the consequences, nor subject yourself to danger and damage.

You deserve better.

No one behaves correctly in their relationships all the time. Everyone makes mistakes, and there's no right or wrong way to live life. There are basics, but there's no instruction manual when it comes to having perfect relationships. However, when a person deliberately hurts another person repeatedly, this is when a relationship becomes abusive. Abuse is a misuse of power intended to harm or control another person (GoodTherapy, 2019). Behaviors from others that focus on creating fear or a bad feeling about oneself are not appropriate and are also considered abuse (1800Respect, 2020).

Types of Abuse

Different forms of abuse have been generally recognized to occur within relationships. Four types of abuse exist (GoodTherapy, 2019; Jared Justice, 2019a; Lancer, 2020):

1.   Physical Abuse: Involves the use of force against the victim. This includes punching, kicking, stabbing, shooting, slapping, biting, etc.

2.   Sexual Abuse: This is defined as the violation of the bodily integrity of an individual, which may involve verbal, non-verbal, and physical behavior. Sexual abuse includes sexual assault, rape, and harassment.

3.   Financial Abuse: Financial abuse involves someone using money in ways to hurt another person. It might include controlling the victim through economic domination or draining finances through extortion, theft, manipulation, or gambling, or by accruing debt in the victim's name or selling the victim's personal property. One of the problematic aspects of financial abuse is that there is no outward showing of the abuse; hence, the victim is entirely at the abuser's mercy.

4.   Emotional or Psychological Abuse: This is a chronic manipulation pattern to control another person (such as who they communicate with and the person). Tactics employed include verbal attacks, intimidation, humiliation, isolation, or threats. A person may also utilize gaslighting to make a target question their memories.

Other Types of Abuse

a)   Verbal abuse - Any derogatory language that abusers use to denigrate or threaten a victim. This includes belittling, bullying, accusing, blaming, shaming, demanding, ordering, threatening, criticizing, sarcasm, raging, opposing, undermining, interrupting, blocking, and name-calling.

b)   Technological Abuse - Similar to cyberbullying. It occurs when a perpetrator uses technology, such as social media, to harass, stalk, or intimidate a victim.

c)   Spiritual Abuse - Spiritual abuse is anything that gets in the way of the victim doing something that causes them to feel great about themselves. More so, spiritual abuse is when a partner does not let the other practice their own moral or religious beliefs or their own culture or values, that is, the use of spiritual or religious beliefs to harm, scare, or control any person.

d)   Manipulation - Indirectly influences someone to behave in a way that promotes the manipulator's goals such that the words seem harmless and even complimentary openly, but underneath, one feels demeaned.

e)   Gaslighting - An act that makes one distrust one's perceptions of reality intentionally or believes that one is mentally incompetent.

f)   Competition – This is contesting to always be on top, sometimes through unethical means, such as cheating in a game.

g)   Sabotage - It is a disruptive interference with one's endeavors or relationships to seek revenge or personal advantage.

h)   Lying – It refers to a persistent deception to avoid responsibility.

i)   Withholding – It includes withholding such things as money, sex, communication, or affection from one.

j) Character Assassination or Slander – This entails spreading malicious gossip or lies about someone to others.

k) Negative Contrasting – Making comparisons unnecessarily to contrast someone with other people negatively.

l) Exploitation and Objectification - It means taking advantage of one for personal ends without regard for one's feelings or needs.

m) Neglect – It is ignoring the needs of a child for whom the abuser is responsible. It includes child endangerment, that is, placing or leaving a child in a dangerous situation.

n) Privacy Invasion - It means ignoring one's boundaries by looking through one's things, phone, mail, denying one's physical privacy, or stalking or following one.

o) Violence - Violence includes blocking one's movement, throwing things, or destroying one's property.

p) Isolation – This type of abuse separates one from friends, family, or access to outside services and supports through control, manipulation, verbal abuse, character assassination, or other abuse means.

Sources of Abuse

Abuse can be from the following sources (1800Respect, 2020):

1. Boyfriends, girlfriends, partners, husbands, or wives

2. Ex-boyfriends, ex-girlfriends, ex-partners, ex-husbands, or ex-wives

3. Carers or paid support workers

4. Colleagues, managers, or bosses

5. Parents, guardians, or other family members

6.   Adult children

7.   Other people: a person they live with or see often, whether inside or outside the home

Emotional and Psychological Abuse

Some people believe that no problem exists if the abuse is not physical. This, of course, is a dated concept, but over the last few years, perhaps a decade, there has been a massive amount of progress when it comes to speaking up about mental and emotional abuse. Some people would refer to the outcome of emotional abuse, including conditions like anxiety, as being mentally weak, but this is an ideal that is thankfully changing.

On top of this, non-physical methods of abuse can end up being much more harmful to the mental health of a victim. Emotional and psychological abuse is both quite different from physical abuse, and although they do not leave physical scars, they can become just as destructive. They result in long-term damage to the victim's mental health.

Emotional abuse is also commonly known as and used interchangeably with the term psychological abuse, also sometimes referred to as chronic verbal aggression. It is any act that includes confinement, isolation, verbal assault, degrading, intimidation, infantile treatment, or other treatment. It's basically any act, process, or action that may reduce the victim's sense of identity, dignity, and self-worth (Tracy, 2012a).

Emotional abuse also refers to the type of abuse that influences someone's feelings, that is, an attempt to govern the other person using the victim's emotions as the weapon of choice. Emotional abuse impairs emotional life and hinders self-growth and personal development. Emotional abuse occurs when resentment starts to outweigh compassion such that there is a translation of the resents—that resentment to harsh words, lack of care, and unfair behavior to one's partner.

Psychological abuse is also referred to as psychological violence or mental abuse. It involves trauma to the victim via various other abusive behaviors used to control, terrorize, and denigrate victims. Psychological abuse aims to manipulate, hurt, weaken, or frighten a person mentally and emotionally, distorting, confusing, or influencing a person's thoughts and actions within their everyday lives, changing their sense of self and harming their well-being (Kaukinen, 2004). Additionally, psychological abuse is usually placed at intervals with warmth and kindness to create emotional confusion, once again returning to that push-pull strategy designed to keep a victim around. Psychological maltreatment can destroy close and trusted relationships, friendships, and even your relationship with yourself. (Tracy, 2012b).

Signs and Symptoms of Emotional and Psychological Abuse

Abusers employ a wide range of hidden tactics to maintain control and brainwash their victims. Some signs and symptoms of emotional and psychological abuse include (Tracy, 2012; Pietrangelo, 2018; Jared Justice, 2019b; 1800Respect, 2020):

I.   Humiliation, negating, criticizing - These tactics are meant to undermine a person's self-esteem such that the abuse is harsh and relentless in both big and small matters. Some common examples are:

a)   Name-calling - The abusers will call the victims all sorts of names, such as "stupid," "loser," etc.

b)   Character assassination - This usually involves the use of the word "always" (such as you are always late, wrong, etc.)

c)   Yelling, screaming, and swearing are methods to cause intimidation and make victims feel small and unimportant.

d)   Public embarrassment - The abusers pick fights, expose the victims' secrets, or make fun of their shortcomings in public or in the presence of family, friends, support workers, or associates.

e)   Belittling victims' accomplishments – Abusers might tell victims that their achievements mean nothing and may even claim responsibility for their success. Instead of congratulatory, abusers take the initiative to belittle victims, whether by ignoring, shaming, or criticizing.

f)   Sarcasm – This entails ridiculing victims such that when victims object, the abusers will claim to be teasing them and tell them to stop taking everything so seriously.

g)   Joking - The jokes might contain an iota of truth to the abusers or be a complete fabrication, all aimed at making victims look foolish.

h)   Insulting victims' appearance – Abusers make comments about victims' looks, such as ugly hair.

II.   Control and shame – This technique aims to make one feel ashamed of one's inadequacies. The tools employed are:

a)   Threats – Threatening to harm a person, the person's pets, children, or other people who are essential in such a way to get the person not to leave them.

b)   Financial control - They might keep bank accounts in their name only and make the victim ask for money when they require it. One might also be expected to account for every penny spent.

c)   Direct orders – This involves issuing orders that are expected to be followed despite their contrary plans.

d)   Digital spying – They might check one's internet history, emails, texts, call logs, and perhaps even demanding one's password leading to a complete lack of privacy.

e)   Monitoring one's whereabouts – The abusers want to know where one is all the time and insist that one responds to calls or texts immediately. More so, they might show up just to see if one is where one is supposed to be. With location tracking services readily available on most computers and smartphones, this is a form of abuse becoming even more widespread.

f)   Treating one like a child - They instruct one on what to wear, what and how much to eat, or which friends to be seen.

g)   Feigned helplessness – An abuser knows it is sometimes easier to do things by oneself than to explain it. Instead, they take advantage of this and say they don't know how to do something.

h)   Unpredictability – They tend to explode with rage out of nowhere, suddenly shower one with affection, or become dark and moody at times.

III.   Accusing, blaming, and denial - This behavior arises from an abuser's insecurities.

They want to produce a hierarchy in which they are topmost, and one is at the bottom. Some examples include:

i.   Blaming one for their problems – Whatever is wrong in their lives is one's fault; hence, they utter words like one is not supportive enough, didn't do enough, etc.

ii.   Jealousy - They accuse one of flirting or cheating on them.

iii.   Turning the tables - They say one is the originator of their rage and control issues by being in such pain.

iv.   Denying something real - An abuser will deny that an argument or even an agreement took place to question one's memory and sanity. This is called gaslighting. It entails telling a person that their actions are crazy or not remembering something correctly or always correcting what a person says, intending to make such a look or feel foolish.

v.   Goading then blaming - Abusers know just how to upset a person such that once the trouble starts, they blame the person for creating it.

vi.   Denying their abuse - When one complains about the attacks of abusers, they will deny it, apparently bewildered at the very thought of it.

vii.   Accusing one of abuse – Abusers blame one for having anger and control issues; meanwhile, they are the helpless victims.

viii.   Trivializing - When one wants to talk about one's feelings that were hurt, abusers accuse the victim of overreacting and manufacturing mountains out of molehills.

IV.   Emotional neglect and isolation - Abusers tend to place their personal needs ahead of their own, thereby trying to come between the victim and their supportive people, ultimately making the victim more dependent on them. They do this by:

a)   Demanding respect - No perceived slight will go unpunished, and you're expected to defer to them.

b)   Shutting down communication – They will ignore one's attempts to converse with them in person, by text, or phone.

c)   Dehumanizing one – They will look away when talking or stare at something else when they speak to one.

d)   Keeping one from socializing - Whenever one has plans to go out, they come up with a distraction or plead with one not to go.

e)   Trying to come between one and one's family – They will tell family members that one doesn't want to attend to them or make excuses for making family functions.

f)   Interrupting – Whenever one is occupied with something, such as being on the phone, etc., abusers get in one's face to shift one's attention to them.

g)   Indifference - They are aware that one is hurt or crying yet, do nothing.

h)   Disputing one's feelings - Whatever one's sense(s) is/are, abusers will point to one as wrong to feel that way or doubt the authenticity of such feelings.

V.   Codependency - A codependent relationship is when everything one does is in reaction to one's abuser's behavior in which one is needed to boost their self-esteem.

You may be codependent if:

a)   You are sad in the relationship, but fear alternatives, such as being alone.

b)   You continuously neglect your needs for the sake of your abuser.

c)   You ditch friends and sideline your family to please them.

d)   You frequently seek out the abuser's approval.

e)   You critique yourself through the abuser's eyes, discarding your instincts.

f)   You prefer living in the present state of chaos to being alone.

g)	You perform a lot of sacrifices to please the abuser but, it is not reciprocated.

h)	You believe that no one else could ever want to be with you.

i)	You feel responsible and take the blame for something done by the abuser.

j)	You feel ashamed when you stand up for yourself.

Effects of Emotional and Psychological Abuse

The impact of emotional and psychological abuse could either be short or long term (Pietrangelo, 2019). Short-term effects are:

a)	Denial

b)	Confusion

c)	Fear

d)	Hopelessness

e)	Shame

f)	Increased heartbeat

g)	Aches and pains

h)	Muscle tension

i)	Moodiness

Long-term effects include:

a)	Low self-esteem

b)	Depression

c)	Anxiety

d)	Chronic pain

e)   Guilt

f)   Addiction

g)   Insomnia

h)   Loneliness

Ending Emotional and Psychological Abusive Behaviors

The steps necessary to stop emotional and psychologically abusive behaviors include (Pietrangelo, 2018; Jared Justice, 2019b):

a)   Work on tackling resentment - Once you have more compassion for yourself, you will be enabled to show more careful thought for the people around you.

b)   Stop rationalizing abusive behaviors - You need first to recognize the rude comments, jealousy, and other actions to finish them off.

c)   Recognizing that an unintentional abuse is still abuse - You may not want to hurt the abuser, but that doesn't mean your behavior is okay.

d)   Accepting that the abuse is not one's responsibility – You should not try to reason with the abuser(s). You may want to assist, but it's unlikely they will break this behavior pattern without professional counseling.

e)   Disengaging and setting personal boundaries – Make a decision not to respond to abuse or get sucked into arguments, stick to it, and limit exposure to the abuser as much as possible.

f)   Exiting the relationship or circumstance - If possible, cut all ties. Make it clear that it's over, and don't look back.

g) Giving yourself time to heal - Reach out to supportive friends and family members; or a teacher or guidance counselor who can help in recovery.

h) Seeking help by speaking with a doctor or mental health professional. They can help work on the inner issues you are having with yourself.

Takeaways

☐ Abuse is when a person intentionally hurts another ceaselessly.

☐ Abuse exists in various forms and through different sources.

☐ Abuse usually entails the words and actions of an abuser(s) and their persistence.

☐ Emotional abuse is also commonly known as psychological abuse.

☐ Emotional and psychological abuse involves someone saying or doing things to make another person feel bad.

☐ Emotional and psychological abuse can happen to anyone (children, teens, and adults).

☐ Signs associated with emotional and psychological abuse are:

a) Humiliation, negating, and criticizing

b) Control and shame

c) Accusing, blaming, and denial

d) Emotional neglect and isolation

e) Codependency

☐ Emotional and psychologically abusive behaviors can have severe and devastating impacts on victims in the long run; hence, impacting the person's ability to parent, work, socialize, and function generally day-to-day.

☐ Both abusive behaviors should be stopped once noticed.

Quick Checklist

1. Are you are being abused at present, or have you experienced abuse-related behaviors? Write down the kind of abuse it is.

_____

_____

_____

_____

_____

_____

2. Write down the impacts (short term or long term) of this abuse on your emotional or mental well-being.

_____

_____

_____

_____

This will help you to know how to tackle this, what to focus on, and work towards total recovery.

Chapter Seven

Gaslighting in Action

"In terms of gaslighting, I define it as the implantation of false and/or distorted narratives that are specially designed or formulated to manipulate a person into a destructive web of deception, loss of control, and the surrender of personal freedom and beliefs of self-worth, self-value, self-esteem, and productivity."
– Ross Rosenberg

Gaslighting in Romantic Relationships

Possibly the most widely recognized utilization of gaslighting is by one accomplice in an intimate and romantic relationship—a traditional couple.

Those in the relationship may demand the rest of the world knows the relationship is loving, and both people involved are close; however, it is not. In reality, the very utilization of this type of control precludes genuine romance and love. The controlling accomplice will start to sprinkle a bit of gaslighting into exchanges at an early stage in the relationship. Maybe the last time you saw them, you consented to do something with each other on the following Monday evening, yet when you raise it later in a chat or on the telephone, they backtrack and say something like:

"Not at all. Silly you, I said Wednesday. I'm occupied throughout the evening on Monday."

This appears as though it is a genuinely honest remark, and it's one you would not question more because you're in the stricken honeymoon stage, and maybe you just misheard or recollected wrong.

Such a thing, in isolation, does not mean you are being gaslighted. It may be that you genuinely did mishear or that they misspoke without having the plans to do so.

However, if this kind of disarray turns into a consistent, regular occurrence, notwithstanding, you have to begin inquiring as to why. Why is this happening, and what is coming out of it? As before, these kinds of mistakes are more than likely to happen every now and then, but if it continues regularly, you may be dealing with a narcissist and gaslighter. As the relationship naturally progresses, you may see further irregularities between what they stated at various points in time. You may recommend eating out at a Chinese place for dinner since they once said they truly enjoyed Chinese cooking. Only, you may get this reaction:

"I'm not a big fan of Chinese cuisine; however, I know an incredible Thai spot we should try."

Is it true that you mixed things up? Was it another person who said they enjoyed Chinese food? Or has there been a transformation in their story between that point and now? As you can see already, you're questioning your reality while trying to figure out what is real and what isn't. This is the crucial bit.

You need to make sure you're not getting drawn into the questioning of asking yourself these questions, but you're instead asking yourself why you're asking yourself these questions. Are you being gaslit? If you think you might be, then it's time to start filling out the checklists found throughout this book, taking time to identify the signs of gaslighting, making a note of the traits of a narcissist, and seeing if you are dealing with one.

Identifying that you are spending your time and becoming attached to a narcissistic person can be scary. On the one hand, you may want to get out of the relationship as soon as possible and run for the hills.

On the other, you may not want to end up alone since you're in a relationship with someone who is treating you well, and you don't want to be mistaken for calling someone a narcissist when they're not. This is why it's so essential to use awareness, look for the signs, and allow time to make your decision from a mindful place before the abuse takes effect.

In the situation that you feel confident the person communicated a preference for one thing just to have them turn to adjust and deny it later on, this could be their method of putting you on the back foot and disgracing you into speculating that you are not focusing correctly, and thus the initiation phase begins.

As the gaslighting is leveled up through into the second phase, the abuser will start to make out that you are beginning to backtrack what you have said in the past. Contingent upon how long you have been a victim, they could legitimately get down on you about it. This is a potential discussion that may occur, one based on my own experiences.

You: "Hey babe, I told my family you'd be coming to our family gathering planned for the end of the month. They are eager to meet you in person."

Gaslighting Partner: "Do you mean that? Didn't we agree that we would hold up somewhat longer before doing the whole family thing?"

You: "Babe, we talked about this recently, and you said you were excited about meeting them too."

Gaslighting Partner: "I said it would be nice to meet them, yes. However, I also proposed we allow for another month. I thought you agreed with me. I suppose it's done now, and I don't want to disappoint, so I'll come."

They presently appear as though they are being obliged by consenting to come, although they had said yes to it initially. This means the conversation's outcome has always remained the same (i.e., they'll meet your family). Still, they have initiated you beginning to doubt your relationship, and the chances are you'll be thinking about this long after the conversation has ended.

Another progression that the gaslighter will take is moving on from responding to your statements or inquiries with lies to beginning discussions with lies about something they have said or done. You may hear something along the lines of:

"Do you recall you said I could borrow your credit card? Well, I recently bought a pair of shoes. I will make sure to pay you back as soon as I can."

This time, they create a discussion where you're allowing access to go through your cash. The abusers realize it did not occur as they have said. You know it did not happen either. Yet, if you attempt to stand up to them about it, they will churn out further lies about how they asked when you were caught up with cleaning up the tiles, and you said it was okay, or some other potentially credible story.

Once more, this is intended to make you question yourself and permit them to attest to power over you and your life, emotions, and assets. When using topics like meeting family or buying shoes, these all seem so insignificant, which is why they can so easily fly under your radar that something is wrong.

As your determination, the stability of your reality, and self-worth debilitates, the victimizer will depend less and less on subtle deceptions and ramp-up to more flagrant lies. They will disclose to you that you or they did (or didn't) do, or something they did (or didn't) accomplish. Perhaps you start running a bath and leave the room to do something else while the water heats up, and the tub fills.

As you return to the room, they have bounced in and claimed your spot. They will demand:

"I came in here a couple of moments back and opened the taps. Maybe you heard me do it and got the thought in your mind that you were the one."

As strange as it sounds, this work of pure fiction is not past the domains of plausibility. Reading the text above, you can so quickly think to yourself, how would anybody fall for that? It's so plainly obvious, but this is how it works. Since you've already been subject to such lies and manipulations in small, seemingly insignificant ways, and you've grown to believe that the abuser is always right, you really start to doubt whether you were the one filling up the bath or not. Each time it occurs, your self-conviction is reduced in little bits, and you arrive at the phase where you question everything. Your brain is letting you know.

Gaslighting within the Family

In a family setting, the most probable bearing for gaslighting to occur is from parent to child. Shockingly, kids are particularly helpless against this type of control because their parent's state generally impacts their perspective. The child knows of no other way of living life and therefore accepts that this is how life is, especially when you add the parent-child bond that cements that this is how families are.

Sadly, children can frequently be subject to violent conduct by one of the two parents, where they may be scolded or rebuffed for something, regardless of whether they were actually at fault. Imagine a situation where a parent and child are late going out for school one morning with no fault at all accrued to the kid; the parent may insist it was their mistake in any case:

"You're going to be late for school thanks to all your messing about this morning. Why couldn't you just keep the peace and do as you were told?"

If words, like the example stated above, are spoken in any event when the kid has done nothing incorrectly, this is gaslighting in action. It shows the youngster that they are irksome and insubordinate, and can't seem to do anything right, regardless of whether they are no more so than some other kid. Over time, this creates the child's self-image, distorting their convictions and impression of themselves, degrading their self-worth and confidence.

Children will generally test the limits set by their power figures, notably, their parents and instructors. This is sometimes referred to as "boundary-pushing" or "limit testing." This occurs from an exceptionally young age and is an essential cycle that trains children on self-control and responsibility, much to parents' distress, of course. Implementing sensible cutoff points is a concrete and essential way of parenting; however, a few guardians are so reluctant to see these rules they have set broken that even the littlest insolence is met with an unforgiving reprimand:

"You are such a devious kid, and I really do not have the foggiest idea of what we will do with you."

Such statements like this just serve to fortify the kid's conviction that they are sufficiently bad and not good enough. All the other kids in the world are better than them, and the best way to be useful is to do exactly what I say when I say it. This is a complete power trip for the parents because the kids will, in time, try to do everything they can to make their parents happy, regardless of how it makes them feel. Like all narcissists, the parents thrive off their children's dependence, which puts them at the top of the family hierarchy.

Whether in family, professional, or romantic relationships, gaslighting does not only make someone question their life experiences, but can also plant the seeds of questions about the very emotions they experience along the way. This is particularly evident in children who are as yet grappling with their feelings and what they mean and have very little understanding of what they are and how to control them.

Imagine the scenario where an adored family dog dies, and the kid is troubled with tears streaming uninhibitedly. Of course, the child is suffering from tragedy and loss, but having never experienced these emotions before, will be naturally learning how to deal with them. In a healthy family setting, the parent will explain what has happened, enforcing that the child is not alone in their way of thinking, and that time will make things better. However, a narcissistic parent may carelessly throw the kid's sentiments to the side by saying:

"Why are you crying this much? You never truly cherished the dog. You never fed it on your own or took it for walks. You are simply acting and constraining some fake tears to get attention. You should be embarrassed about yourself when I am the only person who is remarkably tragic here."

All at once, the parent has wholly negated the child's bitterness, sadness, and all other emotions they are feeling, and even proposed they should feel disgrace for missing the dog. They have likewise educated the kid that it is they, the parent, who is genuinely suffering, is the most important thing and should be focused on at the time. This is regardless of whether the parent actually feels any sense of loss or not. The message is clear: my emotion is what matters; the child's does not.

As a child develops into a youthful grown-up, teenager, and then an adult, the types of gaslighting change considerably. The youngster may have built up some mindfulness that things are not expected, perhaps in the form of resentment against their parents or an underlying gut feeling that something is wrong. Either of their folks is controlling life experiences to their own advantage.

The narcissist parent needs to adjust to continue their needs being met. They may do this by depending less on a complete denial of information disclosed or will continue to attempt to warp their child's reality in any given situation. Expressions like these appear unexpectedly:

"That is not what I implied by any means. You haven't comprehended what I was trying to say. Why are you not listening to me?"

Or on the other hand,

"You are only making up your own story to fit what I have said when it could not possibly be further from the truth."

This kind of comment projects uncertainty in the child's brain about how they have deciphered their parent's words, again making them doubt their abilities to listen and pay proper attention, gradually degrading their worth in themselves.

Romantic partners and friends may come and go every which way as they grow up; however, a parent's significance remains through time since the relationship always has the parent-child bond. The narcissistic parent will understand this, consciously or unconsciously, yet rather than commend and celebrate these significant connections, they will endeavor to use them against the child.

In essence, it means the child will also have some kind of relationship with them and is therefore always available as a means to an end. Gaslighting is one of the methods in which these parents will try to take advantage of this relationship. This involves edging the child to disconnect from those around them, thus falling back into a relationship with the parents. There are endless ways in which this could happen, such as persuading the child, at any age, that their partners and friends do not like them. To do this, they may spout out words like these:

"Do you realize your friends do not generally like you? They are simply using you since you have a car to drive them around anywhere they want."

"John is going to abandon you soon; mark my words. He does not love you. He is only by your side because he sees you are from a wealthy home. And as soon as he is done with you, he will leave your side."

"I heard from Christine that she and your other colleagues just welcome you to parties because they feel sorry for you, as you are pitiful."

"Why do you let Jane treat you so badly? Can't you just open up your eyes for a while and see that she is exploiting you? You have poor judgment in who is a good friend or not."

After hearing these expressions and others like them, the child may start to doubt whether these statements are valid or not. Regardless of whether they realize their parent to be a manipulative liar, it may be hard not to let their remarks not be taken personally. Similarly, with all gaslighting, every comment, remark, and statement plant the seeds of uncertainty. In some cases, it will develop and obliterate a relationship essential to the youngster in that time of their life.

We already touched upon how memories can be utilized to confound somebody in a romantic relationship, and the equivalent can occur in a parent-kid setting. The problem this time is that the child may have been too young to remember correctly, so they have to rely on what their parents say.

A parent can exploit this by successfully retelling an occasion and demanding that the "realities" were unique to what they are saying, rather than being whatever the kid thinks happened. For instance, they may say something like the child has a sibling who once got in trouble in school for fighting with their classmates. The parent may choose to say:

"You caused me endless headaches when you were much younger. I used to get called into school since you were caught fighting. I was so humiliated."

The kid may feel absolutely sure that it was their sibling who stumbled into difficulty, yet it was quite a while ago during their childhood, so perhaps they could have remembered it all wrong?

On the off chance that they attempt to correct their parent, they will almost certainly be met with a quick and firm dismissal of this point from the parent. They may say something like:

"All things considered, your sibling was older, and you were only a kid, so obviously, they recollect it better than you do."

When a child grows up, gaslighting is frequently utilized by the parent to protect themselves and demonstrate that they are and were a decent parent. This could include retelling the past or lying about the present. Let's say, for instance, that the kid is presently a parent themselves, and this discussion comes up:

Child: "You never said how charming your grandkid is."

Parent: "That is nonsense; I state how cute he is constantly."

The parent needs to say this since, well, they would appear as though a quite awful parent and grandparent if they didn't, and this isn't something they are ever going to admit. It is a fundamental lie; however, it again puts the kid on the back foot since it's hard to prove.

As much as the examples in this section allude explicitly to a parent-child relationship, with parents being the gaslighter and the kid, the gaslightee, it can also be the other way round, most especially with adult children and aging parents. Also, gaslighting can include any relatives—siblings, aunts, uncles, cousins, grandparents, or far-off relations; there is no restriction to when and how it can happen.

Gaslighting at Work

Whether it is a colleague or the boss, it is conceivable to wind up being gaslighted within any work environment. Frequently utilized as a strategy to acquire or maintain control, it can drive you to surrender if you let it and don't see the gaslighting attempts for what they are.

Let's say in the wake of being approached to play out a specific obligation X, whether that's working on a new project or handling a new client, and you report back to your manager that the task is done, just for them to answer:

"Why have you been burning through your time on that job when I told you to do this one?"

Naturally, you get somewhat unsettled by this and attempt to defend yourself, only for you to be probably confronted with a response such as this:

"Wouldn't you say you're overreacting just a little bit?"

Here's another example. Imagine you were guaranteed a raise after a specific measure of time working at the company. At the end of that speculated time, nothing was done about it, and when you bring it up with your boss, he says,

"I never said I would give you a raise. I only said I would consider it depending on your job performance, which remains fairly average."

Afterward, there's the partner in the company who's conspiring to get a promotion ahead of you who will coolly drop a portion of these accompanying lines into the discussion to sabotage your confidence and make you question your value with regards to climbing up the profession stepping stool:

"I heard the supervisor wasn't satisfied with that report you sent him. Somebody's in a tough situation!"

"Is it true that you weren't in that email? I guess the supervisor doesn't confide in you with such information yet. Maybe you'll get there one day."

"I just said you have to up your game a little. Jeez, somebody's somewhat sensitive today!"

It can be activities, interactions, or just words that structure the gaslighting actions. Possibly they turn off your PC screen while you're away from your work area or move some hardware to a different place, denying that anything has changed when you return.

Now, these are the main forms of gaslighting that you may find throughout your life, and anybody can be affected by them from anyone at any time. However, while these may be seen as the most "traditional" forms of gaslighting, they are not the only types, as you'll see below.

Racial Gaslighting

This form of gaslighting occurs when people or individuals apply gaslighting techniques to some other group of people depending on their race, skin color, or ethnicity. They may say:

"The Blacks are not experiencing any sort of discrimination from the whites."

Or,

"You civil rights activists are too emotional to undermine our message. Can't you just see things the way they are?"

Even though the evidence is saying otherwise, they choose to say what they believe is the reality of the situation, thus planting doubt in your mind.

Medical Gaslighting

This gaslighting occurs when a medical practitioner or a doctor dismisses or trivializes an individual's health concerns based on the assumption that they are mentally deranged. They may tell the persons that the symptoms they are feeling are their imagination and not real, which is entirely untrue.

This form of gaslighting can happen both in a professional setting (perhaps by a doctor, narcissist therapist, etc.) or by a family member, colleague, friend, or loved one.

Political Gaslighting

Political gaslighting occurs when a political figure or group uses deception, denial, or manipulation of information to control people. This has sadly become commonplace in mainstream politics as of late. I'm not one to say whether political figures like Donald Trump gaslights (I personally avoid politics like the plague), but many certainly believe that he does.

Examples of political gaslighting include actions like being secretive about their administration's wrongdoings and choosing to deny fault when problems are brought up or surfaced. Political figures may discredit their opponents based on mental instability, using controversial issues to divert people's attention from essential occasions (which is a very recent claim between Donald Trump and Hillary Clinton).

Remember, gaslighting is intended to befuddle you and cause you to feel unreliable, and this can take various structures.

In some instances, the disarray is amplified utilizing one primary method. We have already explored some cases where the abuser talks their victim down, causing them to appear to be neglectful or powerless, or lacking. However, on the off chance that these were consistently the situation, the victim would attempt to escape the relationship—regardless of whether from an accomplice, work, or family.

This is why, to forestall this from happening, the abuser may hear and put up an appealing, benevolence, and cherishing conduct. What this does is it keeps you (the victim) hoping for a positive result. Remember how we said earlier that flagging your partner as a narcissist can put you in an awkward situation? Sure, you may not want to be with this person, but it's better than being alone, and if you're wrong, then you may be missing out on a beautiful situation. It's hard to know what decision is best.

When an abuser catches on to the fact you're going through this decision-making process, they will begin the push-pull process. If they feel you slipping away or wanting to leave, the narcissist will start showering you with affection and showing you how great the relationship can be. It's almost like saying this is what you're missing out on if you leave, so why are you choosing to leave?

This kind of behavior shows you that things aren't all that awful and that you can stick things out for one more day. It has a symptom that is similarly amazing with regards to confounding the person in question. By being lovely now and again, the victimizer plants further seeds of vulnerability into your mind. Rather than recognizing what's in store, you will perpetually stay uncertain of how things are going to be each and every day, leaving you in this near-constant state of anxiety. Will today be a pleasant day or a cold-blooded day? What can I do to make things as pleasant as possible? This is particularly common in a romantic relationship where "love" as a concept is what is holding you (the victim) in subjugation to your partner (the gaslighter).

Takeaways

This chapter provides practical examples of scenarios where gaslighting is seen in action. It talks about:

Gaslighting in romantic relationships

Gaslighting in the family

Gaslighting at work

Racial gaslighting

Medical gaslighting

Political gaslighting

Quick Checklist

Take an in-depth look at all the relationships you are in. Can you make a list of some statements that have been made to you concurrently that made you confused, question your reality, or doubt yourself?

_____

_____

_____

_____

_____

_____

Highlight those who have said those things to you and what type of relationship you are in with them.

_____

_____

_____

_____

_____

_____

Ask yourself, "Do these people often do or say things that make me confused or doubt my reality?" This would help you know how you can deal with gaslighting in such relationships, as you cannot handle all of them the same way.

In the next chapter, we will be discussing toxic relationships and why these kinds of relationships have so much effective power over you.

Chapter Eight

Toxic Relationships and Why They Affect You

"Don't let negative and toxic people rent space in your head. Raise the rent and get them out of there."-Robert Tew

One of the essential decisions an individual can make is to be in a relationship; the second most basic is with whom not to be in a relationship with (White-Cummings, 2016).

Every single phase of your life includes relationships of some kind, and most importantly, those relationships' attributes are huge components that impact our mental and enthusiastic well-being. Simply put, if you have quality relationships with the people around you, you're more like to have a good quality of life. Many people say that you are the average of the five prominent people you surround yourself with. If you surround yourself with positive people who work hard and make their dreams come true, you'll tend to do the same. On the other hand, if you are down-trodden, abused, or around addiction-orientated people, you might lean in that direction.

A straightforward approach to deal with sorting relationships as positive or negative covers the genuine practices that happen in your life. Individuals in your life could regularly limit or completely disregard risky and dangerous actions or experiences that compromise the physical, mental, and emotional well-being. But what defines as risky or damaging is subjective to each and every individual and the experiences we've had as we've grown up through life, making it difficult to define and therefore flag what a toxic relationship is solidly.

Telling a lady that she's in an "awful" relationship with her life partner doesn't make half as much impact as helping her see that the emotional manipulations and physical animosity she's encountering are abuse.

Saying to a male companion that his relationship with his mom isn't "sound" is not as groundbreaking as showing him that consistent deception, escalating arguments, and manipulations are poisonous at the root. Being told you're in a toxic relationship is as much of a life-changing revelation as the individual seeing for themselves that they're in a toxic relationship.

Imagine a mother who gets pulsating headaches whenever she needs to deal with her daughter, foreseeing the regularly unreasonable pushback she will get in light of even the most straightforward remark. Suppose she can realize that what she is encountering with her daughter is past the ordinary rubbing between a parent and kid.

In that case, this can highlight the fact that she may have an unhealthy and toxic relationship with her daughter. On the other hand, she may live in denial, claiming that all daughters are like this to an extent, and "it is what is it," meaning she's never going to be proactive in trying to make the situation healthier.

Toxic relationships can be challenging to characterize, and here and there, toxicity can be entirely subjective (based on an individual's opinion), not necessarily by ticking points off a checklist.

However, toxicity in a relationship is known as being a blend of behaviors that are both brought about by toxic reasoning and toxic feelings to those included. In other words, if you feel like there's something wrong in your relationship, there probably is, even if you can't quite put your finger on what that something wrong is.

Seemingly the most destroying thing about toxic relationships is that they trap their victims and abuse. Most of the time, the victims in a toxic relationship will have seen both sides of the same coin. On the one side, the relationship can be beautiful and fulfilling. The sense of connection can be so strong, seemingly like no other relationship the individual has ever been in.

On the other side of the coin, there is such a deep-rooted pessimism towards the relationship. Physical symptoms like tension, stress, headaches, depression, anxiety, and fatigue are all present. The individual may feel completely physically and emotionally exhausted, even after the most minute of interactions with their partner.

Over time, these toxic relationships can lead to further sentiments of low self-esteem, powerlessness, dread, nervousness, misery, uncertainty, distrustfulness, and even narcissism itself.

Gaslighting is just one of the many signs that showcase you could be in a toxic relationship. As with gaslighting itself, you may experience the signs and symptoms of a toxic relationship here and there in every relationship you're in. After all, we are all human beings. However, suppose you notice these signs consistently throughout your relationship. In that case, it could be indicating you're in a toxic relationship and will need to start thinking about what you can do about it.

Indications of a Toxic Relationship

A quality relationship can give us the affection, friendship, security, and caring we desire, and having these relationships are essential to our life satisfaction as human beings. However, not all connections benefit us.

At our very cores, everybody has an idea of what a toxic relationship is, or at least what it looks like, and how entering into one is perhaps not a smart idea. Yet, it's common for people to end up in toxic relationships regardless. This is because the beginning of a new relationship is promising and exciting. Naturally, when we meet someone new and get on with them, our brain awards us with serotonin and dopamine to make us want to continue investing in this relationship. As time goes on, these bonds strengthen, and we come to rely on these hormones and chemicals to tell us we're happy. However, in a toxic relationship, we might be feeling anything but happy.

There is a psychological concept known as the "sunk-cost investment." In laymen's terms, this refers to the idea that the more you invest in something, the harder it is to get out of. If you have a business idea, let's say a coffee shop, you may pour a ton of resources into getting it off the ground, mainly time and money.

Yet, there may, unfortunately, come the point where the business idea isn't working out, and it's time to call it a day before you invest more of yourself unnecessarily. However, since you've already invested so much, you want more than anything to make this business idea work, so you invest more and more until there comes an explosive point where you can't invest anymore, and it all falls apart, leaving you more destroyed than if you had pulled out months ago. The same concept applies to relationships.

There is an emotional and spiritual cost to leaving and cutting ties with any relationship, even if you're fully aware the relationship isn't doing you any favors. It's difficult to concede that your loved ones don't adore you back in the manner that you need, aren't providing for your needs, and aren't providing the satisfying and fulfilling relationship that you truly deserve. Acknowledging you are in a destructive relationship can feel like your reality is tumbling down, and as you're reading this, then chances are the thought has already crossed your mind before.

How did you react? Did you scare yourself with the thought? Did you want to push the idea away and try to never think of it again? In any case, recall this is your life and that you are encircled by acceptable individuals—regardless of whether you have been stuck in a hurtful relationship for quite a while. Say, for instance, you became hopelessly enamored with somebody who's absolutely stunning, and the relationship is going incredibly. You can't believe your luck, and you're sure you've met the one. The rest of your life has begun, and it's going to be beautiful. And then, it all seems to fall apart without warning.

You need to accept the individual you have decided to be with can't take the blame no matter what. You may tell yourself repeatedly that they would never hurt you and only set out to find what's best for you, just like you are doing for them. Unfortunately, this isn't, in every case, valid.

Are you beginning to feel your relationship probably won't be sound much longer, and does something inside you tell you this is an extreme idea or concept to address? Don't worry, every relationship goes through a rough patch here and there. Those are necessary for a relationship to grow stronger. However, check out these signs to consider if your relationship with an individual is or has become toxic to see if it's something you need to think about addressing:

1.   Absence of Respect

Indeed, you know about this! Every human deserves respect no matter who they are because every human, even narcissists, are living their lives trying to do the best they can with what they have. Yet, when considering toxic relationships, we regularly twist and warp our genuine meaning of respect. Respect implies that your suppositions, thoughts, and ideas are unmistakably esteemed. In a toxic relationship, there is next to no or no regard for your emotions and feelings. You are caused to feel that you are not significant in settling on choices in the relationship—or worse, that your thoughts shouldn't be voiced by any means. If you feel like what you have to say or think doesn't matter, this is a huge indicator of a lack of respect.

2.   Absence of Effort

Do you find there is a distinct lack of effort towards the relationship from your abuser? Do you feel helpless with regards to taking a shot at your relationship? Do you try bringing up solutions to problems you're experiencing, only for them to get shut down or dismissed? Does your partner not listen to your needs or deny any problems are happening at all?

Your abuser may demand making attempts to make things better and for you both to seek happiness and a more content relationship; however, on the off chance that you don't feel it, think about whether everything is only in talks. Remember, actions speak louder than words, so look for your partner's actions, not focusing on what they're saying.

An example of this from my own relationship came in the form of spending more quality time together. My ex-partner and I were falling into habits where we would always be doing our own thing, whether that was simply reading books, watching TV, binging Netflix, and so on. It was unsatisfying because we were basically just two people sharing a house, not a couple who were in love.

So, to try and revitalize that spark, we planned date nights. Starting with once every other Friday, and hoping to move to a weekly basis, we planned to do something, whether that was going to the cinema, going for a meal in a restaurant, going to a Christmas fair, and so on.

While my partner seemed very excited and enthusiastic about doing all this, I planned several dates, but he couldn't find the time for them. I asked if he wanted to plan something, and he didn't. While his words said he wanted to try, his actions said otherwise.

3. Lies and Dishonesty

In a toxic relationship, dishonesty increases gradually and exponentially.

It may start off small, and maybe subtle things you don't even notice, whether they're gaslighting you or just can't be bothered to have a conversation. They might say something like:

"I didn't read your text? Oh, I was busy at work," when really they were just watching YouTube videos, saw your message, but couldn't be bothered to respond.

"I've got a headache. Let me relax, and you cook dinner," when you could be doing it together.

Of course, these lies can occur on the extreme end of the scale. Suppose your partner is hiding an addiction, such as having affairs, watching porn, drinking excessive amounts of alcohol, or taking drugs. In that case, the lies will become even more speculative to hide what they're really up to.

4. Absence of Trust

You undergo questioning regarding everything, and this is a surefire sign that your partner is toxic, controlling, paranoid, and perhaps even trying to manipulate you. You might hear questions like:

"Where are you?"

"Where exactly are you going?"

"Who are you with?"

"Did you leave your desk at any point?"

"When will you be home?"

"What were you doing in the bathroom?"

These are routine questions that can be asked at any time by anyone. However, they go beyond the ordinary when they become constant or when certain conditions follow them. Conditions, for example, whom you can see, and whom you ought not to meet any longer, places you cannot visit, and so on.

5. Absence of Effective Communication

As much as you may be involved in talks that are not too personal or less significant, you may find yourself unconsciously, perhaps consciously, ceasing to disclose substantial and in-depth information to your partner. Perhaps the victimizer stays away from circumstances and conversations that require talking, regardless of whether they need talking about, or you've actually requested that you sit down and talk. You may also find yourself questioning yourself when you address your partner and could even be too frightened to disclose anything to them, based on intense experiences you've had when you've tried talking to them in the past.

6. A Wide Range of Abuse: Verbal, Emotional, Physical

The toxic relationship ordinarily advances from serene to all-out maltreatment. It starts off pleasant and exciting enough, but it won't take long to see toxic symptoms. First comes the compulsive verbal abuse, perhaps using the controlling methods we spoke about previously or by lying to you. Next, the victimizer may disparage you and call you excessively delicate for "acting" harmed, especially if you've shown the confidence to express how you feel and air that you don't think things are right in the relationship (i.e., you're not being treated how you deserve to be treated). You may find there are accompanying gaslighting statements such as "You are insane, you are crazy, and you have lost it!" No inquiry: tossing out such charges talks more about their psychological state than yours.

After or alongside verbal abuse can come physical terrorizing, which can transform into plain power. There's a touch of pushing and getting pushed around, perhaps a smack that you pardon in light of the current situation. Finally, this can lead to all-out physical maltreatment, where your body bears the abuser's savagery. You may wind up wounded, in the hospital, and even scared for your life in extreme circumstances.

Please note that if you find yourself in this situation, you need to leave the relationship and seek help. I understand this can feel very difficult and that there are few escape options. I can't give complete advice once again because every relationship and situation is different, but if you can, make sure you go and stay with friends or family and resolve to get out whatever it takes. It may seem impossible now, but in the future, when you can look back and realize how things were and how much happier you are free and being confident in yourself, you'll realize for yourself that the hardship of leaving was worthwhile.

It seems many of us wind up in this position without even acknowledging it. Remember, it is not your fault you're being terrorized or abused. It's a reflection of the person you're with. There is no shame in being the survivor of abuse, only become strengthened by learning how to protect yourself from it happening again in the future. And if it does? Well, there's just another lesson to be learned and an experience to grow from. However, you can stop the toxic relationship before it comes to physical maltreatment. You owe yourself that.

7. Latent Hostility, On Either Side

The relationship turns into a latent forceful one, meaning you both keep a psychological record of fights and arguments, scorecards, and conflict with each other and every possible turn. At that point, you begin accusing and questioning each other for all that matters with the relationship. Without a lot of hard work and letting go of past resentments, usually with a professional counselor's aid, the relationship won't be redeemable.

Harmful Effects of Toxic Relationships

Humans long to interface with everyone around us and have a place with something greater than ourselves. It's instinct to be part of a social group. It's hardwired for our survival.

Let's say you lived back in caveman times when we drew on walls and hunted for food. If you were alone, the chances are you wouldn't survive long. If you were ill or injured yourself, there would be nobody to look after you, or to go and get the food, or to do a million of the other jobs necessary to live and thrive.

However, as a group, if you were injured or sick, someone could look after you, and you could do the same for them. You'd have enough hours in the day to get everything done, and that's how we got to where we are as a civilization today. It's part of our natural evolution to be social creatures and to interact with one another. That's the feeling of loneliness you may sometimes feel. It's your instinct telling you to go out and interact with people.

However, we don't live in small tribes anymore but can connect with literally millions of people, all in one go. With that, we spend such a large amount of our lives attempting to discover our place on the planet. It makes us feel connected to be validated and accepted by someone else, regardless of whether it is an inappropriate individual.

Relationships can be a dubious thing to explore, and love is frequently a feeling too confusing even to begin thinking about trying to understand. At times, relationships turn poisonous without importance, and we probably won't perceive the broken examples and elements we have with somebody until it's past the point of no return. That is why we have to put forth a valiant effort to recognize what's solid and what's not beneficial in a relationship and stop a toxic relationship before it does an excess of harm for us ever to fix.

With that said, here are some adverse impacts that an unhealthy relationship can have on your life:

1. Toxic relationships force you to remain on the lookout

There's no denying that our history affects the present, and the experiences we've gone through in our lives shape the person we are right here in this very moment. This means the relationships you've had in your past are going to shape how you feel about relationships. For example, if you've been cheated on in past relationships, then unsurprisingly, you're probably going to have some trust issues when it comes to future partners.

In this situation, your encounters with toxic relationships may make you warier and more suspecting of others, meaning you may hold back when it comes to developing new relationships. You become anxious about the possibility that if you get excessively close to somebody, they will hurt you again like you've been hurt before, so you hold back and don't fully invest yourself.

You may assemble dividers around yourself and become more protective of your feelings. However, in doing such, you are setting all your future relationships up to bomb by regarding them as though you are simply sitting tight for them to commit an error to then give you a reason to leave.

The more this happens, the more you're validating your own beliefs that relationships are toxic and will never work again, and the snowball effect once again comes back into play.

2.   Toxic relationships make you more cynical

Have you just cut ties and finished things with your abuser?

Your perspective on the world and point of view changes in the wake of being in a toxic relationship. Where there was once hopefulness and happiness—an exciting new chapter of your life—these feelings have maybe been replaced with feelings of tension, dread, and doubt.

You may become critical towards adoration and new connections and could even separate yourself from people around you who you are already close to out of fear of being let down. You are additionally liable to battle with sentiments of blame, dejection, and different types of emotional troubles that typically follow a separation.

You may start to look at the world from a position of nervousness, anticipating that everybody should act like your harmful accomplice. You may again feel that nothing can satisfy you and that you cannot do anything right. What's more, you begin to loathe things you recently did. That sort of mental injury is challenging to get over, and it can remain with you even after you have proceeded onward. It may take months or years, but this will get better in time as long as you're mindful of what is going on.

If you're lost in your pain, it can be tough to find your way out again.

3.   Toxic relationships breed pessimism

Hand in hand with the point above, it's difficult to be glad when you feel as though you're stuck in a toxic relationship. You regularly feel like there's a dull downpour cloud tailing and overhanging you any place you go, making you see the most noticeably awful thing in yourself, your day, your circumstance, and pretty much everything else in your life. You are continually feeling awful because investing such a significant amount of energy with somebody so negative will cause you to develop a hostile demeanor. And how could you not? If you're always on guard, always feeling like you have to defend yourself, and continuously having bad days, of course you're going to start thinking life sucks.

4.   Toxic relationships genuinely debilitate you

Harmful connections are sincerely depleting because you invest such an extensive amount of your time, energy, and vitality devoted to making the other individual glad and satisfying their needs rather than your own. You feel restless and worried when you invest energy with this individual since they are narcissistic, excessively condemning of you, and they make everything about them. They suck you into such a large amount of their silly show that, on certain days, simply being around them is depleting.

A great test to see if this affects you is simply seeing how you feel whenever you're around them. Let this be your reminder to try, and trust me, even reading this now is a great way to nudge your brain into thinking about it when you're next around your partner. Take a moment to check in with yourself. Are you feeling tense and uneasy? How do you feel? How does just talking about them make you feel? Can you feel the stress and tension? All of this is worth taking note of because it's your body showing you how you really feel.

5.   Toxic relationships annihilate your self-confidence

The connection we have with others and how we allow them to treat us says a lot about how we feel about ourselves. In fact, many consider the company we keep being one of the most significant establishments of an individual's mental self-portrait. When you're in a toxic relationship with somebody who couldn't care less about you, it's hard not to feel awful about yourself.

If you're continually in a position where you're denied the adoration, backing, and consolation you look for, and it will, without a doubt, truly negatively affect your confidence. You lose certainty, quit having faith in yourself, and battle to feel self-esteem when you're in a toxic relationship. You will feel like your psyche, thoughts, and feelings have been at war. You may encounter sorrow, and you will feel intellectually depleted.

6.   Toxic relationships inhibit your personal development

When you are trapped in the web of a toxic relationship with somebody, there is very little space for you to develop yourself. From various perspectives, with the help of gaslighting techniques, they might even change you to be more terrible than to improve things.

Since you quit thinking for yourself because the other individual consistently attempts to control you and command you, you let them persuade you that you are sufficiently bad to get what you need. You shouldn't try to improve or get better. You're convinced that you're okay just where you are, even though that is supposedly a bad place where you're unhappy, and they will fool you into believing that you need them and you're nothing without them.

7. Toxic relationships contort your concept of a healthy relationship

One of the most noticeably awful ways a toxic relationship can hurt you is by causing you to accept that you merit it. Being abused and exploited by somebody you once thought such a significant amount about twists your concept of what a relationship ought to resemble. You may unconsciously disguise your agony to the point where it begins to feel natural. You will search out likewise hurtful and useless connections since it is what you feel generally comfortable with. After some time, you will lose your capacity to perceive when an upbeat, solid relationship tags along.

8. Toxic relationships contrarily influence your health

While unmistakably toxic connections are incredibly hurtful to your emotional well-being, you may be astounded to discover that it can also negatively influence your physical well-being. Studies show that harmful relationships regularly bring about more dangerous effects, such as heart issues, higher glucose levels, blood pressure, and a debilitated resistant framework, slowing wound healing. Weakness and low vitality are expected, given the stress and uneasiness that many people in poisonous relationships experience consistently (De Vogli et al., 2007; Powell et al., 2013; Slavich et al., 2014).

<u>Takeaways</u>

Throughout this chapter, we discussed what toxic relationships are, and that gaslighting is a technique employed in unhealthy toxic relationships as it aids in the weakening of the victim's mental health and compromises the relationship's stability involved.

We also discussed some of the signs that reveal you are in a toxic relationship are:

i.   Absence of respect

ii.   Absence of effort

iii.   Lying

iv.   Absence of trust

v.   Absence of effective communication

vi.   A wide range of abuse: verbal, emotional, physical

vii.   Latent hostility, on either side

Also, we talked about the harmful effects of toxic relationships:

i.   It makes you hypervigilant

i.   It makes you more cynical

iii.   It breeds pessimism

iv.   It genuinely debilitates you

v.   It annihilates your self-confidence

vi.   It inhibits your personal development

vii.   It contorts your concept of a sound relationship

viii.   It contrarily influences your health

<u>Quick Checklist</u>

Do you think you are in a toxic relationship, be it at work, in your marriage, a romantic relationship, friends, or parents?

From the indications listed in this chapter, write down the frequent signs you see in your relationship that makes you think it is toxic.

_____

_____

_____

_____

_____

What are the effects of these toxic individuals around you having in your life?

_____

_____

_____

_____

Do you think you cannot escape these individuals because that partner or job is very important to you? The next chapter reveals how you can deal with toxic relationships. Follow it through, and you are on your path to freedom and living your life peaceably.

Chapter Nine

How to Deal with Toxic People

"Toxic relationships are hazardous to your health; they will literally kill you. Stress shortens your lifespan. Even a broken heart can kill you. Your arguments and hateful talk can cause you to find yourself in the emergency room or in the morgue. You were not meant to live in a fever of anxiousness, screaming yourself hoarse in a frenzy of dreadful, terrifying fight-or-flight that leaves you worn out and numb with grief. You were not meant to live like animals tearing one another to shreds. For your own precious and beautiful life and for those around you — get help or get out before it is too late. This is your wake-up call!"— Bryant McGill

Dealing with Toxic Individuals

Toxic individuals make no sense.

Some are willfully ignorant of the pessimistic effect they have on everyone around them, and others appear to get fulfillment from creating turmoil and pressing people's buttons. In any case, they create pointlessly unpredictable experiences, difficulty in day-to-day life, and most exceedingly terrible of all, generate pressure and anxiety where it doesn't need to exist.

To deal with toxic individuals adequately, you need an approach that empowers you, in all cases, allowing you to control what you can or find peace with what you can't. The significant thing to recall is that you are in charge of far more than you perhaps realize, and part of your recovery journey will be about understanding what you can and can't control. I'm a firm adherent that toxic emotional episodes (like junk mail) ought not to be perpetrated on one individual by another, under any conditions. So how might you best deal with the fallout from others' persistent toxicity? Let's find out.

1. Move on with your life without them

If you know someone who ruinously demands control and creates the emotional atmosphere you've grown tired of, at this point, be clear: they are toxic. If you are in distress due to their disposition, and your sympathy, tolerance, counsel, and general mindfulness doesn't appear to support them, it's time to get real and start thinking of the real action you can take. You have it in your power to do so. It's at this point you need to ask yourself, "Do I need this individual in my life?"

When you decide to erase a toxic individual from your environment, you become significantly more relaxed. Only choosing to start working towards a better, happier, freer version of yourself will already get your mind working in a way that aims to set you free, no matter how it is you need to go about this and what loose ends you need to tie up. If the conditions warrant it, desert these individuals, and move on when you can.

Truly, you have got to be strong, and yes, I know, it's easier said than done. It's going to take a tremendous amount of courage to take this action, but you'll look back and feel amazed and so confident in yourself that you had the power to do it. You believed in yourself, and you did what was right, which is looking out for you and putting your well-being first. Let them know that nothing more will be tolerated! Relinquishing toxic individuals doesn't mean you disdain them or wish them to hurt; it essentially implies you care about your prosperity and want to thrive on your own energy for a while.

Don't worry if you don't feel like now is a good time and you need some time and space to think it over. While I'll first remind you that the longer you stay in a toxic relationship, the harder it is to get out, you need to figure out what works for you and move on in your own way.

Remember, a good relationship is reciprocal; it ought to be an even series of giving and taking, yet not as in you are continually giving, and they are always taking. However, if you must genuinely keep a toxic individual in your life, regardless of the reason, consider the following points.

2.   Set boundaries

Boundaries are essential in any relationship. I've said it before, and I'll say it a million times more. Boundaries. Boundaries. Boundaries. The main problem with negative individuals is that they unload all their negative energy all over everyone else who will listen and bear it. Usually, they don't feel the slightest bit of remorse or guilt in doing so. They want individuals to join their pity party so they can be at ease thinking about themselves. It's validating how they feel and say that it's okay. Of course, it's okay to feel sad at times and want to share and talk through things with a friend or loved one, but that's very different from actively bringing someone down, support being completely one-sided, and using you as an emotional or supportive punching bag. You are not a sink for destructive emotions and energy to be poured down!

Individuals frequently feel strain to tune in to complainers since they would prefer not to be viewed as callous or inconsiderate. Yet, there's a barely recognizable difference between listening closely and getting sucked into their negative emotional winging.

Fortunately, you can separate yourself from absorbing the negative energy by setting boundaries and creating limits. If your abuser wants to complain and unload a ton of negativity onto you, but you're not able to support them, then you need to say, "I can't deal with this right now." Can we talk about it later? Of course, since you're not gaslighting them, you will be available to speak to them later. If they're bitching and moaning about people at work, family, or friends, and you don't like how that person is speaking about these other people, you need to voice how you feel. If you don't and let it slide, you're allowing this kind of conversation to be acceptable.

Consider it this way: if the complainer were smoking, would you decide to stay there, breathing in the recycled smoke? If you don't smoke, you would probably distance yourself, and you ought to do likewise with whiners and toxic people. An excellent method to set boundaries is to ask the whiners how they plan to settle the issue they're moaning about. They will either calm down or deflect.

Setting limits will prepare you to ponder when and where you need to endure them and don't. For instance, regardless of whether you work with somebody intently on a task in a group setting does not imply that you have to have a similar degree of one-on-one cooperation with them that you have with other colleagues. You need to find what works for you.

You can develop a limit, yet you'll need to do so deliberately, concisely, and proactively, mostly if you haven't done anything like this before. If this is a first, then it's probably going to take the toxic person by surprise, but hold your ground and stick to doing what you believe is right. It may take some practice, but you'll get there with experience.

If you allow things to carry on as normal, you will undoubtedly wind up continually involved in troublesome discussions. If you set boundaries and choose when and where you'll connect with a problematic person, you can control a significant part of the chaos. The major stunt is to stand firm and keep limits set when the person attempts to infringe upon them, which they will. Genuinely toxic individuals will pollute everybody around them, including you, on the condition that you permit them. If you have attempted to reason with them and are not yielding, don't spare a moment to abandon their space and overlook them until they do. Relationships work both ways. They should respect you just as much as you respect them.

3.   Don't give up; keep fighting

I understand that everything we've spoken about in this book is a lot to take in, and even if you're reading it and adopting the strategies here over time, then it's still a lot to handle and requires a considerable amount of change in your life. Once you start putting things into action, you are literally changing your life from everything you already know, and that's scary. It's frightening. You don't know what the future holds, which can make you want to stay where you are now, even if you know it's not a good place to be.

However, you must not give up trying to live the life you want to live.

Effective individuals realize that it is imperative to live to battle one more day, mainly when your enemy is toxic. In conflict, unchecked feelings make you get down to business and face the sort of conflict that can leave you seriously harmed. At the point when you peruse and react to your feelings, you're ready to pick your fights admirably and possibly persevere when all is good and well.

4.   Rise above them

When you're in a toxic relationship, it's easy to see, usually with hindsight or the help of an outside perspective, that the relationship is about the other person, not you, and not about both of you as equals. You have got to know this. Toxic individuals make you insane because their conduct is so unreasonable. Furthermore, because the "guilty" feelings that loom, or even the suggestion that we may have accomplished something incorrectly, can hurt our certainty and agitate our determination.

Beyond a shadow of a doubt, their conduct conflicts with reason. So, for what reason do you permit yourself to react to them genuinely and get sucked in with the general mishmash? The more nonsensical and misguided somebody is, the simpler it ought to be for you to eliminate yourself from their snares. Stop attempting to beat them unexpectedly at their own game.

Distance yourself from them emotionally and approach your relationships like they're a science task (or you're their therapist). You don't have to react to the emotional disorder—just the realities. What your abuser says and does, and the suppositions they have, depend altogether on their self-reflection.

5.   Don't allow anyone to limit your joy

At the point when your feelings of delight and fulfillment are formed and obtained from the assessments of others, you are not at peak bliss. Whenever you feel good about something you've done or accomplished, or even just enjoyed, you should not let anybody's feelings or inconsiderate comments remove that happiness from you.

I remembered vividly one day when I worked hard on a client project for about a month, and I decided to allow myself a lazy day—just snacks and Netflix and not much else. My partner came home and called me lazy, disgusting, and couldn't believe what I was doing. I was so upset at the time, and I took what he said to heart. I look back and wish I had stood up for myself because I enjoyed my day, and it gave me the reset and break I needed to get the project done to the best of my ability. Not that I should have to justify my actions to anybody, let alone to a toxic, self-centered person like him!

While it is difficult to turn off your responses to what others consider you, you don't need to liken yourself to them. Remember, people only think in a way that resonates and reflects how they feel about themselves. For example, if my ex is getting upset because he thinks I'm lazy, that's a reflection of him and how he feels about himself. It's not something I should take personally because it's just his way of viewing things, which isn't necessarily the right or correct way. It's only one way. Regardless of what the toxic individuals in your life are thinking or doing, your self-esteem originates from the inside. Despite what individuals think of you at any given second, one thing is for sure: you're never as positive or negative as it is commonly said you may be.

6. Quit pretending that their toxic conduct is all right

If you are not cautious, toxic individuals can utilize their testy conduct to get special treatment since it just appears to be simpler to calm them down than to tune in to their cranky manner of speaking and then try and resolve things. Try not to be tricked into this way of thinking because being toxic is not acceptable. Just to note, it's okay to be toxic and have a bad day now and then. Someone in your life might just have had a bad day and need to sleep it off, meaning they're going to be cranky and upset in the meantime. As emotionally immature and unstable as it is to take those feelings out on you, we're only human, which will happen at times. However, just like gaslighting, if someone is consistently and frequently toxic, then you've got a problem.

When someone is toxic and breaches the barriers and limits you've set, it's time to lay down the law and declare this isn't acceptable. A relationship is a two-way thing, and it's completely unfair to be treated in such a demeaning way.

7.   **Shout out!**

Constant antagonism is never worth enduring. If somebody over the age of 21 can't be a sensible, dependable grown-up, you're well within your rights to find an ideal opportunity to speak up. A few people will do anything for their benefit but to the detriment of others: cut in line, take cash and property, menace and put down, pass blame, etc. Try not to accept this manner of conduct. The more significant percentage of these people realize they are doing an inappropriate thing and will back down shockingly immediately when stood up to. In most social settings, individuals will, generally, stay silent until one individual decides to speak up.

When addressed, especially when addressing a narcissist in public, they may get outraged and freak out. This causes a scene and makes everyone feel awkward and not want to do that again. This is understandable but remember that you're not speaking up to upset or embarrass the individual, but rather stating that what they're doing and how they're acting is unacceptable. This isn't easy. When you start speaking up, the individual will either go on the defensive or even attack you with something that matters to you to hurt your feelings and divert the negative attention onto you instead of them.

If at any time you set out to speak up and react antagonistically to their irritable conduct, they might be shocked, or even offended, that you've intruded onto their social region. Be that as it may, you should never allow yourself to be silent about this; stand up for yourself. Not acknowledging somebody's toxic conduct can turn into the chief purpose behind being sucked into their psyche games. Testing this sort of conduct forthright gradually and over time will get them to understand their behavior's negative effect. For example, you may state:

- "I have seen you appear to be furious. Is something the matter with you?"

- "I think you look exhausted. Do you think what I'm stating is not necessary?"

- "Your behavior is upsetting me at the moment. Is this what you're trying to achieve?"

Direct statements like these can be disabling if somebody utilizes their moody demeanor to invoke social manipulation. These announcements can likewise open an entryway of chance for you to attempt to support them if they are genuinely confronting a significant issue that needs to be addressed. You're getting two birds with one stone here because it neutralizes negative behavior and allows for positive support to take place if required.

Regardless of whether they ask what you mean, deny there's anything wrong at all, change the subject, or accept your request for support, the end result is that you've made them mindful that their attitude has become a known problem to another person, as opposed to only an individual apparatus they can use to control others at whatever point they need.

8.   Be practical with practicing compassion

At times, it bodes well to be thoughtful with toxic individuals you know are experiencing a troublesome time or the individuals experiencing an ailment. Like I said, if someone is having a bad day, sure, let them be a bit toxic and in a bad mood. I personally believe there are other ways of dealing with things, but it's subjective. Let's say your partner loses a parent, and they're very upset about it, which has resulted in them being a bit toxic and resentful towards life; it is understandable why they are acting the way they are.

There is no doubt that some toxic individuals are troubled, discouraged, or even intellectually and genuinely sick; however, despite everything, you need to isolate their authentic issues from how they act toward you. If you let individuals say things that you take personally, you allow the negative energy to spread when it doesn't need to. It should instead be contained and handled as an individual issue. Someone else's problems in life are not a reflection of you.

I heard a story of a doctor, Dr. Marc, who volunteered at a psychiatric hospital for children several years ago. He mentored a child there called Dennis, who was diagnosed with bipolar disorder. Sometimes, Dennis was a handful and would frequently yell vulgarities at others when he encountered one of his episodes. However, nobody at any point challenged his upheavals, and neither had the doctor so far. He's got a condition, and therefore that explains the outbursts, right?

One day, he took Dennis to a nearby park to play catch. An hour into their field trip, Dennis found himself in one of his episodes and started calling the doctor profane names. Rather than overlooking his comments, he stated, "Quit tormenting me and calling me names. I know you are a pleasant individual, and far more superior than an individual who only calls people bad names." His jaw dropped. Dennis looked paralyzed, and afterward, very quickly, he gathered himself and answered, "I'm sorry I was mean, Mr. Marc."

You can't "help" somebody by causing ridiculous exculpations for all they do just because they have issues. Several people are experiencing outrageous difficulties are not toxic to everybody around them. We can act with authentic sympathy when we set limits. Making such a large number of negative outbursts isn't sound, reasonable, or beneficial for anybody in the long haul.

9.   Set aside time for yourself

If you are compelled to live or work with a toxic individual, ensure you get enough alone time, and find ideal opportunities to unwind, rest, and recover. Assuming the role of an "engaged, sane grown-up" even with toxic grumpiness surrounding you can be debilitating and, frankly, utterly exhausting. In the event you're not cautious, the toxicity can enter your being and taint you. Once more, comprehend that even individuals with authentic issues and clinical ailments can grasp that you have needs too, which implies you can amiably pardon yourself when you have to. You merit this time away to recharge and refresh your state of mind.

You have the right to think calmly, liberated from outer weights pushing down on you and toxic conduct: no issues to explain, limits to maintain, or characters to please. Here and there, you have to set aside a few minutes for yourself, away from the bustling scene you live in. Your discretion, consideration, and memory are diminished when you don't get enough—or have the correct kind—of rest. Lack of sleep raises pressure levels and changes in hormones. A decent night's rest makes you more sure, inventive, and proactive in your way to deal with toxic individuals, giving you the point of view you need to be able to manage them.

10.   Remain mindful of your feelings

Keeping up an emotional separation requires mindfulness.

You can't prevent somebody from pressing your buttons if you don't perceive it when it's going on. Now and again, you will wind up in circumstances where you will have to pull yourself together and pick the ideal path forward. You need to choose how you want to respond to specific situations, not just getting carried away with your emotions and letting them take you over unconsciously.

Consider it this way: if an intellectually unsteady individual comes across you in the city and reveals to you that he's John F. Kennedy, you're probably not going to sort him out. At the point when you wind up with a colleague who is occupied with similar crashed reasoning, most of the time, it's ideal for grinning and gesturing only. In case you're the person it falls upon to need to fix them, such as whether it's a loved one, it's smarter to give yourself some time to think when the ideal opportunity is to approach the subject and sort out the issues from a balanced place, not a time when emotions consume you.

11. Utilize your emotionally supportive network

It's enticing, yet altogether insufficient, to endeavor to handle everything without the help and support from anybody else. To manage toxic individuals, you have to perceive the shortcomings and develop your own way of dealing with them. It's very easy to get lost in the emotions of it all, so having back up, an outsider's point of view, and someone to discuss ideas with can be make or break as to whether your attempts to make things right will work.

Yes, you're allowed to talk to the people you care about and let your emotionally supportive network in to help and receive a greater perspective on a problematic individual you're trying to deal with. Everybody has a co-worker and people outside work in their social group who can be counted upon for preparing to support you to get the best out of a troublesome circumstance.

Recognize these people throughout your life and put forth an attempt to look for their understanding and help when you need it. Something as straightforward as opening up about the situation you're in can make a world of difference and may inspire you tenfold with their unique viewpoint. More often than not, others can see an answer that you can't because they are not as emotionally committed in the circumstance as you are.

Enduring the ups, downs, and lightning storms of others' moodiness can be a significant challenge. However, it's crucial to remember that some irritable, antagonistic individuals might be experiencing a troublesome phase in their lives. They might be sick, incessantly stressed, or lacking what they need regarding love and passionate help. Such individuals should be tuned to, upheld, and thought about (albeit whatever the reason for their grouchiness and pessimism, you may, in any case, need to shield yourself from their conduct now and again).

Some of the time, removing individuals from your life may appear the best way to get away from their toxic conduct. However, this is not typically done. If you need to invest energy with somebody who displays harmful behavior, remind yourself their activities aren't your shortcoming or your obligation. Significantly, they demonstrate what you're not ready to endure.

Takeaways

In this chapter, we explained how you could deal with toxic people in your life in detail. Although these poisonous individuals only use gaslighting as a technique, not all toxic people are gaslighters, but all relationships where gaslighters are involved are unhealthy. Ways to deal with toxic individuals whom we discussed are:

i. Move on with your life without them

ii. Set boundaries

iii.   Don't give up; keep fighting

iv.   Rise above them

v.   Don't allow anyone to limit your joy

vi.   Quit pretending that their toxic conduct is all right

vii.   Shout out!

viii.   Be practical with practicing compassion.

ix.   Set aside time for yourself

x.   Remain mindful of your feelings

xi.   Utilize your emotionally supportive network

Quick Checklist

What are your encounters with toxic individuals?

_____

_____

_____

_____

_____

Reflect on the ways we have discussed above that can help you in dealing with toxic individuals. Write down how you plan on following through with those points. Be very practical, specific, and as feasible as possible.

_____

_____

_____

_____

_____

Make a list of the emotionally supportive people around you that you could call on and open up to if you need to.

_____

_____

_____

_____

_____

Recognizing these people throughout your life and accepting their help would go a long way in helping you deal with these toxic individuals.

It would be ideal for sharing your thoughts by writing your responses; this will help you voice your concerns.

In the next chapter, we will be discussing the various ways you can overcome gaslighting in your relationships.

Chapter Ten

Overcoming Gaslighting in Relationships

Gaslighting is a common tactic in emotionally and physically abusive relationships, and it's a betrayal of essential trust (Gattuso, 2019).

Dealing with Gaslighting Parents

Well, here we are. It's been one hell of a journey through the realms of gaslighting. We've learned everything there is to know, from what it is, where it comes from, why it happens, what to look out for, how to deal with it, and what you can do to prevent toxic people from coming into your life. However, there's one final bit to tackle, and that's how to actually recover, move on, and overcome your gaslighting experiences.

Suppose one suspects that one's mother or father (or both) is gaslighting one. In that case, the steps necessary in putting an end to the manipulation are as follows but can be applied to any relationship in which you're experiencing gaslighting in action (Bennett, 2018; Stebar, 2019):

1.   Confide in a trusted individual about the manipulation: A child can go to a trusted adult, perhaps at the place of worship or school, and describe some of the things that bring concern. As an adult, you'll need to think about being able to go to a trusted friend or family member that you can openly talk to about what you're experiencing.

2.   Maintain healthy boundaries: A child may need to establish firmer boundaries with parents to prevent them from impacting one negatively. It is also always advisable to have less contact (or no contact) with parents where possible and necessary if it would help. The same applies to adults. You need to make sure you're setting boundaries or considering what your boundaries are and what is and isn't acceptable in a relationship with you. You can think of boundaries as being the minimum level at which you want to be treated.

3.   Talk with a psychologist or professional counselor about one's concerns: Counseling can help repair the family if possible. The child can enter psychotherapy or counseling, or the whole family can be seen to help change this unhealthy dynamic. Perhaps, if the parents know that it is hurting their child, they will hopefully stop their acts; however, this is unlikely because most parents do not view such actions as problematic behavior.

4.   Visiting a family therapist to potentially correct this unhealthy dynamic: Though complicated and involving lots of courage, it is important to discuss or uncover your parent's manipulative behavior with a professional.

Dealing with Gaslighting Friends

While facing gaslighting as a child comes with its own range of pros and cons, the same applies when dealing with gaslighting among your friend and social groups. Some of the best ways to combat friends' manipulation include (Bennett, 2018b; Gil, 2019; Econotimes, 2020):

1)   Understanding the severity of gaslighting: First and foremost, one must realize this emotional manipulation tactic's seriousness as gaslighting is used to help the manipulators or gaslighters get their way every time. The fact is that gaslighting is severe and not a game;

hence, you should not allow a friend to gaslight one. Look for consistency and regularity in your friend's actions.

2)   Set firm boundaries: No matter how minor the gaslighting from a friend may seem, it is paramount to set healthy boundaries as soon as possible (such as not borrowing from them, not entrusting your children or pets to them, etc.) and inform such friends about the negative impacts of their behavior to you and the boundaries you would enjoin them to respect if the friendship must progress. If they oppose your decision, then it is a clear indicator that they value neither you nor your mental health, and that's hardly a friendly behavior. This is where you'll start to figure out whether this is something you actually want in your life.

3)   Give them time to adjust: You may find out that your friend is going through some stuff at home or is trying to grow as an individual, which means you could actually support their recovery journey, rather than just cutting them out of your life. If friends show respect and a genuine effort to uphold your decisions and respect your point of view, it is safe to say they value your presence in their lives and genuinely want to put effort into your relationship. Hence, it's a good idea that gives them some time to adjust to your new boundaries. Just keep an eye on what is happening to make sure they are actually putting effort in. Remember, actions speak louder than words.

4)   Recognize patterns of behavior that don't change: Whatever caused your friend(s) to start gaslighting could be out of their control and beyond your understanding, but that still doesn't make it acceptable. Therefore, you must keep an eye on those subtle behaviors that don't seem to change to prevent a doorway for more significant manipulation. Note that gaslighting has a snowball effect, and the longer you stay in it, the more severe it tends to become.

5)   Make a tough decision: The most challenging part of a relationship is knowing when to end it. This is a mature and weighty decision to make but must be made at some point. You can't simply put up with it forever. When they don't follow or respect one's boundaries, you might need to step away from the relationship. This could involve staying away (that is, cutting all ties with them) or acting bored or ambivalent such that they walk out first.

6)   Consult a professional: Finally, if you are unsure about a particular friendship or need some additional guidance when dealing with them or moving on, you should consider talking with a mental health professional or a therapist, as friends can sometimes be skewed in their opinions.

Dealing with Gaslighting at Work

Gaslighting in the workplace can be difficult since you spend so much of your life there, and it's a very public space where you'll have managers and colleagues from all walks of life around you. However, several steps can be taken in dealing with a gaslighting boss, employer, etc., which include (Burry, 2019; Sarkis, 2020):

I.   Get grounded in your truth: Gaslighting is all about distorting your sense of reality. This means it's necessary to sit with what you know to get yourself back, grounded in reality, once experiencing gaslighting. Trusting yourself is the key to coping with this toxic behavior and identifying what's real and what isn't. Pay attention to what the gaslighting is telling you, so you know what you potentially doubt yourself about.

II.   Keep documentation: Once you feel gaslighted or harassed at work, it is necessary to keep documentation of memos, emails, dates, times, people involved, direct quotes, and other evidence proving what is happening. Do not keep this data on a work-issued device, as the company may have access to that data and will take the device upon quitting the job or may have access to the files to manipulate. You can't simply believe that a manipulator won't do this. One should not trust one's memory as verbal proof and is nowhere near as impactful as digital or paper forms of evidence.

III.   Ask colleagues if gaslighting is also happening to them: Sometimes, a gaslighter(s) at work will focus their abuse on one employee, but they often see many people in their path to power and will gaslight them as well along the way. Therefore, it is good to find out the gaslighter's interactions with colleagues. If they also receive similar treatment, one could ask them if they are willing to document the gaslighting behavior. This helps one from being the only one making a complaint since strength lies in numbers.

IV.   Do not meet with a gaslighter alone: You must be very cautious of private meetings with gaslighters; instead, you must consider bringing in a trusted co-worker or another supervisor as a witness. If the gaslighters refuse to allow another person in the room, ask for the reason and tell them of your uncomfortable feelings. Additionally, if you have to meet with a gaslighter alone, you must ensure proper documentation.

V.   Know your rights: You should learn your workplace protocol (if any) for reporting harassment. An attorney, especially one specializing in workplace rights, can give you legal advice and recommend what steps you should take to guard yourself and if you have a potential harassment case against your employer.

VI.   Consider leaving the job: Yes, it is unfair to quit your job due to someone else's deplorable behavior. Yet, it is vital to think about what it costs you emotionally and regarding your mental and physical well-being, as we've discussed in previous chapters. Exiting the gaslighting situation and looking for something else is sometimes the best option.

Dealing with Gaslighting in a Romantic Relationship

Ending any romantic relationship is never easy, and perhaps the hardest breakup of all is with a gaslighter because as you're leaving, they pull you in, and once you're back in, they push once again, keeping you in a state of limbo. However, these are the steps to take to deal with gaslighting in a romantic relationship that can help things get better, or can help you leave entirely and start working on building a new chapter in your life (Burry, 2018):

A.   Break up in one quick conversation: If you're choosing to break up with your partner and simply want to get out and move on, the key to a successful separation is making it fast and precise. Tell the gaslighter that the relationship is not working, and as such, it is over in a straightforward, calm, and direct voice. Also, try to avoid language that offers an opportunity to make alternative decisions that the gaslighter may use to change your mind. Believe me, they will try.

B.   Don't believe promises to change: Immediately, as you put a halt to the relationship, your former partner may try to win you back by tendering instant apologies and promises that things will change with words that sound authentic and genuine. They'll try and remind you of how beautiful the relationship was at the beginning and what you're potentially missing out on. A part of you might want to believe them. However, it is all part of the manipulation, and you should not give in to their words or pleas. The unhealthy relationship dynamics will return and, perhaps, get worse. If you've tried to make things better several times and it turns out the abuser isn't changing, or even putting effort into growing, then it's time to call it quits and get out.

C.   End all communication: Once the relationship has been ended officially, cease all means of communication (such as blocking their phone numbers, emails, accounts on social media, not picking up calls from unknown numbers, etc.). They may also try to enlist mutual friends in their effort to reunite; you must tell them to desist from discussing the gaslighter, and if they refuse, you may need to simply walk away from the conversation.

D.   Ask friends to remind you of how bad things were: Even when you know breaking up was for the best, you might still grieve the end of a relationship that seemed so promising. With things like social media, it's sometimes hard to avoid people. You may see a picture and start doubting whether you made the right choice, and perhaps you want to go and see if they're going to try the relationship again. This is when depending on your loved ones, social circles, and support groups come in. When thoughts of giving the victimizer a second chance creep into your head, your support network will remind you of the horrible past and that you deserve better. In the absence of friends and family, group therapy (helps you realize that you are not alone in situations like this) could be beneficial. You can even flick back through this book or through the notes you've made to remind you of everything you wrote down and how you felt. One excellent technique I saw one lady using was that she walked away and wrote a letter to herself at the end of her relationship. She wrote about how awful she felt in the abusive relationship and how empowered she felt finally walking away. Whenever she had the idea to reconnect, she reread the letter.

E.   Make a list and check it in moments of doubt: Hand in hand with the letter-writing idea above, a simple checklist can help dramatically after a breakup. Write down all the times you felt gaslighted during the relationship and read through it whenever doubts about just how poisonous the relationship was or when hopes

167

of reconciling arises. The list will remind you that the relationship was unhealthy and unworkable and reaffirm your commitment to stay away from them forever.

Dealing with Gaslighting in Marriage

It may not be pleasant to deal with a gaslighting spouse—you may even tend to ignore such a partner—but if you notice it early, the following tips can make dealing with it much easier (Valecha, 2020; Smith, 2020) and will help you have the power to make your own decisions and protect your well-being:

a)   Respond to their malicious claims immediately: Arguing with a gaslighter is vain because they'll gaslight at any given opportunity and conveniently make it look like whatever it is you're talking about is your fault. More so, a gaslighting partner is never going to understand your side of the argument. In order to survive gaslighting, you need to tell your partner patiently that your experience of their claim is not the same as theirs, and you'll need to stick to your guns while doing it. Yes, I understand this may seem hard, but you are strong and powerful, and once you've done it before, so there's no reason you can't do it again. Think of it this way...if your partner really loves you and cares about you (as you would expect and deserve in a loving relationship), they will hear you out and want to discuss and understand your point of view, and not dismiss it as a gaslighter does. Offer to sit them down and talk about it. Sure, the chances are your partner is going to be defensive and angry but, being sensible and straightforward through it all might have a calming effect on them.

b)   Second-guessing is not an option: Dealing with a gaslighting spouse can be overwhelming, but you must have confidence in yourself. At any given claim of a gaslighting spouse, it is essential to pause and think if what they are accusing you of is actually true. There is a massive difference between your belief and what you are being pressured to believe; therefore, understanding the distinction is vital in surviving gaslighting. Make sure you're keeping proof of things that are happening if you suspect gaslighting to be taking place, so you can check and have a sound state of mind.

c)   Keep yourself grounded at all times: A gaslighting spouse will tear down your sense of thought and foundation to lose your idea of individuality and engage in their games of manipulation. Therefore, you need to keep yourself grounded and not let your spouse's hints, doubts, and gossip shake the belief in yourself and everything around you. Having control of your emotions and thoughts can help you deal with a gaslighting spouse better. Mindfulness meditation and journaling are a fantastic practice since you're literally training yourself to be grounded in the calmer times, which allows you to remain grounded during the stressful times where you may be experiencing heightened emotions.

d)   Closely focus on the accusations: Seeing if there is any credibility in what a gaslighting spouse is throwing at you will aid dealing with such accordingly. For example, if you are being accused of cheating on your partner or bold claims are being made that you're lying to them, all you have to do is take a step back and analyze if you have done anything to incite those accusations. If not, then the chances are that your partner is the one who is engaging in the act, and this will give you a better grip on the situation and help you deal with the gaslighting spouse.

e)   Confront them with the problem: A gaslighting spouse may pretend like they are listening. Eventually, they'll blame it on you or that have been misunderstanding things, and that all their accusations and other gaslighting personality behavior were simply out of care and concern. If your spouse is in complete denial of their behavior and does not attempt to understand or change, which is the most important in your marriage, it may be time to let go.

f)   Seek professional help if things get worse: A counselor or therapist will help you see your relationship's downfall in a better, more productive manner and even guide you with some strategies to deal with your gaslighting spouse. They will also help you rebuild your confidence, walk you through grounding yourself better after the relationship has ended, and even help you reconnect with your true, genuine self.

g)   The last resort to deal with a gaslighting spouse is to leave them: if you have tried everything and can't make any progress, then it's time to leave and let go. As we said above, choosing to leave any kind of relationship can be a tough decision to make, especially with things like the "sunk-cost" investment, which means the longer you've been in the relationship, the harder it will be to leave because you've already invested so much of yourself into it. However, sometimes things in a relationship just can't get better. There's too much negativity in the past, too much resentment towards each other, and too many built up, habitual emotions that you'll both need time and space to let go of. Quitting a marriage can be a bit of a process, but if it's the right thing to do, then know that you're taking a bold step into a new and happy life that you can build for yourself.

Defending Yourself against Gaslighting

Of course, regardless of where you're experiencing the gaslighting abuse in your life, several tips are important to remember if you're looking to defend yourself, protect your emotional and mental well-being, and keep yourself in a sound state of mind. (GoodTherapy, 2018):

a.   Recognize the abuse is present: This is often the first step to protect yourself from gaslighting. After all, you can't fix what you don't know is broken. Once you are aware of being manipulated, you can determine your reality more quickly.

b.   Don't take the blame for the other person's actions: The other person may claim you provoked the abuse and that it's all your fault ("You made me act this way"), but it's important not to give in to their claims. You are never making someone else act a certain way. Even if you make someone so angry on purpose, they still always have a choice in how they operate, just like you do. If you should avoid the actions that offended them in the past, the gaslighter will likely develop new excuses for their abuse.

c.   Don't sacrifice yourself to spare their feelings: The other person's desire for control will never be fulfilled, even if one dedicates their whole life to ensuring their happiness. People who gaslight others are usually trying to fill a void in themselves, but they will not fix their hearts by breaking yours.

d.   Remember your truth: The mere fact that the other person sounds sure of themselves doesn't mean they are correct. It's just a good performance. The gaslighter may not ever see your side of the story yet; their thoughts do not define reality, nor do they explain who one is. Their view on life, just like everyone else's, is subjective to them and is usually a reflection of how they see themselves.

e.   Do not argue on their terms: You are unlikely to have a productive discussion if the other person is fabricating facts. You may expend all your energy, claiming what is real instead of making your point. The abuser may use gaslighting techniques to declare that they have won an argument, but you do not have to make conclusions based on a defective premise.

f.   Prioritize your safety: Gaslighting usually makes targets doubt their intuition, but if you have a feeling of danger, you can always leave the situation. You do not need to prove that a gaslighter's violence threats are sincere before reporting to the appropriate place. It is often safest to treat every risk as credible.

g.   Remember, you are not alone: You may find it helpful to talk about others' experiences. Friends and family can offer emotional support and validation. Also, therapy is a safe place where you can talk through your feelings and memories without judgment. A therapist can help to recognize healthy and unhealthy behaviors, teach you how to resist psychological manipulation, and in some cases, help to develop a safety plan for leaving the relationship.

Takeaways

☐   Gaslighting in relationships is always gradual and slow.

☐   Recovering from gaslighting is not an easy task, but it's worth the work it takes.

☐   The more confident one is in one's beliefs, the easier it will be in dealing with a gaslighting person.

Quick Checklist

1)   Examine your life to check whether you are undergoing gaslighting.

_____

_____

_____

_____

2)   To what extent have you been gaslighted, and what have your coping strategies been?

_____

_____

_____

_____

3)   Check how far you have gone in recovering or overcoming gaslighting from parents, friends, relationships, marriage, and the workplace, and tick the appropriate box.

	Parents	**Partner**	**Marriage**	**Work**
Not Recovered				
Slightly recovered				
Minimally Recovered				
Fully Recovered				

4)   Write down the extent to which you have been able to defend yourself from being a gaslighting target.

_____

_____

_____

_____

_____

_____

Conclusion

"The gaslighter avoids responsibility for their toxic behavior by lying and denying and making you question facts, your memory, and your feelings. Basically, the gaslighter makes you feel crazy and confused." –Karen Salmansohn

To be trapped in the narcissistic snare of trickiness and deception is comparable to being a fly caught in the cobwebs. When entering the web, does the victim realize that it will be bound up and eaten alive by anything other than the fly? The appropriate response is "no."

Deciding to move on and leave the web does not mean you don't cherish your partner, boss, or parent. It implies you esteem reality and are more passionate about opening the door for you to be more joyful, more confident, and surer of yourself as an individual, regardless of whether it implies separating. The ill thing about gaslighting is that it takes place more regularly than you might expect.

What's more, it works so well that you would be astounded to discover that scholarly and straight-thinking individuals fall victim. Your relationship with this individual that once appeared as though paradise has now ended up being terrible, and it's something that nobody wants to admit, making it even harder to accept.

There is no harmony or euphoria living your life in this position, when all that is left inside you is a constant dread and unending desire for concealment. Your life has lost all expectations, and, as though the light has been killed, all you see around is murkiness and the profound dark haze of melancholy. You are currently compelled to live in a condition of passive consent to endure.

The gaslighter's deception constantly subverts your perspectives on the truth, so you wind up losing trust in your instinct, memory, or thinking powers. These are spun lies that disclose to them that they are over-delicate, envisioning, absurd, nonsensical, over-responding, and reserve no option to be vexed. Their existence is turned back to front upon hearing this on numerous occasions, and they start to accept this may all be valid.

The narcissist's form of psychological abuse and oppressive practices has figured out how to ingrain in their victim the extraordinary feelings of uneasiness and disarray to where they no longer trust their memory, recognition, or judgment. In this state, they are a prisoner. Nonetheless, many can figure out, usually with a bit of help and guidance, how to discover and obtain the fortitude to break free.

Yet, these are generally after a few problematic endeavors. Yet, when they do at long last break, they may discover their way to the therapy room in time. Remaining in a toxic relationship can break our spirits. However, acknowledging that you deserve a better relationship where you are treated as worthy and receive the level of respect that you and all human beings deserve? That's liberating.

You fully deserve and have the right to be in a stable relationship where you are regarded and treated with affection. You ought to never need to bargain for somebody who doesn't treat you right. There is another person out there who is more suited to providing for your needs and will aim every day to treat you better.

More critically, delayed toxic connections can have enduring, negative consequences for our psychological wellness, constraining us to feel useless or irrelevant. Given time, you'll be able to release these negative feelings and reverse the effects, but you need to find the courage to take that first step.

I'm hoping you've found this book useful, and it's giving you absolutely everything you need to identify, highlight, overcome, recover from, and deal with gaslighting in your life, and basically how to deal with any kind of toxic relationship you may find yourself in, both now and in your future.

I've tried to include everything you need to regain your reality and power, and you will be in a position to be able to realize the narcissist at work and be equipped to guard yourself against further re-victimization. And I wish you all the very best in the future.

Do not underestimate the power of recovery; the fact that you have survived such extreme abuse up until this moment is proof of your strength and determination. I never fail to wonder at the resilience of the human spirit. I unequivocally recommend that you take action, as discussed in this book. See a professional who can help you pinpoint what's going on and design tactics to protect you, keep a record of discussions (in writing if possible), or include third persons to have other ears in the conversation. Be proactive, stop the madness, and you will be able to get on with living a happy and secure life.

Thank you!

Before you go, I just wanted to say thank you for purchasing my book. I poured a ton of time into this book and shared a lot of my personal experiences and those of people I spoke to when compiling the book to show you that you're not alone in this, and a beautiful and fulfilling life where you can feel safe and free from abuse is within your grasp.

You just need to reach out and make it happen. Every journey, even one along the road to recovery, starts with a single step. This is your permission to take yours.

It's also a fantastic thought to me that you could have picked from dozens of other books on the same topic, but you took a chance and chose this one.

So, a HUGE thanks to you for getting this book and for reading all the way to the end.

Now I wanted to ask you for a small favor. Could you please consider posting a review on the platform? Your reviews are one of the easiest ways to support the work of independent authors, and it's incredible to go online and see all the amazing support this work has received. I love hearing from you, and hearing your feedback inspires me to write more in the future and helps me to identify what to do better and how to be the best writer I can.

This feedback will help me continue to write the type of books that will help you get the results you want. So if you enjoyed it, please let me know! (-:

Lastly, don't forget to grab a copy of your Free Bonus e-book "*7 Essential Mindfulness Habits*"!

Also by Amy White

Digital Minimalism in Everyday Life: *Overcome Technology Addiction, Declutter Your Mind, and Reclaim Your Freedom*

How to Declutter Your Mind: *Secrets to Stop Overthinking, Relieve Anxiety, and Achieve Calmness and Inner Peace*

Beginning Zen Buddhism: *Timeless Teachings to Master Your Emotions, Reduce Stress and Anxiety, and Achieve Inner Peace*

References

1800 Respect, (2020). Psychological Abuse. Retrieved on September 4, 2020, from https://www.1800respect.org.au/violence-and-abuse/psychological-abuse

Bain, L., (2019). What is a Narcissist? - 8 Key Traits of Narcissism Everyone Should Know; GH. Retrieved on 27 August, 2020, from https://www.goodhousekeeping.com/what-is-a-narcissist/

Bennett, T., (2018a). Are my parents gaslighting me?- Here's what to do if your parents are Manipulative and making you feel self-conscious, anxious; Thriveworks. Retrieved on September 9, 2020, from https://thriveworks.com/blog/combat-gaslighting-friends/

Bennett, T., (2018b). Are my friends gaslighting me?; Thriveworks. Retrieved on September 9, 2020, from https://thriveworks.com/blog/combat-gaslighting-friends/

Burry, M. (2018). How to Break up with a Gaslighter; Health. Retrieved on September 9, 2020, from https://www.health.com/relationships/breakup-gaslighter

Burry, M. (2019). Are You Being Gaslighted at Work? Here's What to Do About This Dangerous Form of Abuse; Health. Retrieved on September 9, 2020, from https://www.health.com/condition/anxiety/gaslighting-at-work

Cleveland Clinic, (2020). Narcissistic Personality Disorder. Retrieved on 27 August, 2020, from https://my.clevelandclinic.org/health/diseases/narcissistic-personality-disorder

De Canonville, C.L., (n. d). The Effects of Gaslighting in Narcissistic Victim Syndrome. Retrieved on 27, August, 2020, from https://www.goodtherapy.org/blog/psychpedia/gaslighting

De Vogli R, Chandola T, Marmot MG., (2007). Negative Aspects of Close Relationships and Heart Disease. Arch Intern Med. 2007;167(18):1951–1957. doi:10.1001/archinte.167.18.1951

Dean, M.E. (2020). Gaslighting: A Sneaky Kind Of Emotional Abuse; Medically Reviewed by Horn, A. Retrieved on 30 August, 2020, from https://www.betterhelp.com/advice/relations/gaslighting-a-sneaky-kind-of-emotional-abuse/

Dodgson, L. (2018). There are 3 distinct types of narcissists — here's how to spot them; Business Insider. Retrieved on August 31, 2020, from https://www.businessinsider.com/how-to-spot-different-types-of-narcissist

Econotimes, (2020). How to Handle Your Friend Gaslighting You. Retrieved on September 9, 2020 from https://www.econotimes.com/How-to-Handle-Your-Friend-Gaslighting-You-1580087

Ellis, M.E. (2020). Separating the Myths from Facts about Narcissistic Personality Disorder; Helix Treatment Centers. Retrieved on 30 August, 2020, from https://www.helixtreatment.com/blog/separating-the-myths-from-facts-about-narcissistic-personality-disorder/

Gattuso, R. (2019). How to Spot — And Heal From — Gaslighting; The Talkspace Voice. Retrieved on September 8, 2020, from https://www.talkspace.com/blog/gaslighting-in-relationships-signs-how-to-spot/

Gil., N. (2019). Gaslighting Happens in Friendships Too. Beware of these Signs; Refinery29. Retrieved on September 9, 2020, from https://www.refinery29.com/en-gb/2019/03/224570/abusive-friendship-gaslighting

GoodTherapy. (2018). Gaslighting. Retrieved on September 10, 2020, from https://www.goodtherapy.org/blog/psychpedia/gaslighting

GoodTherapy. (2019). Abuse/Survivors of Abuse; GoodTherapy. Retrieved on September 7, 2020, from https://www.goodtherapy.org/learn-about-therapy/issues/abuse

Gulla, E. (2020). What is Narcissistic Abuse and How Can You Get Help?; Cosmopolitan. Retrieved on September 2, 2020, from https://www.cosmopolitan.com/uk/love-sex/relationships/a32851018/narcissistic-abuse/

Hutson, M. (2015). The 2 Faces of Narcissism: Admiration Seeking and Rivalry; Scientific American Mind. Retrieved on September 1, 2020, from https://www.scientificamerican.com/article/the-2-faces-of-narcissism-admiration-seeking-and-rivalry/

Jared Justice. (2019a). The 5 Main Types of Domestic Violence. Retrieved on September 2, 2020, from https://www.jaredjustice.com/the-5-main-types-of-domestic-violence/

Jared Justice. (2019b). The Difference Between Emotional and Psychological Abuse. Retrieved on September 2, 2020, from https://www.jaredjustice.com/blog/the-difference-between-emotional-and-psychological-abuse/

Kaukinen, C. (2004). Status compatibility, physical violence, and emotional abuse in intimate relationships. Journal of Marriage and Family, 66(2), 452–471. Accessed on September 4, 2020, from https://safelives.org.uk/psychological-abuse

Kritz, F. (2020). What Is Narcissism? Symptoms, Causes, Diagnosis, Treatment, and Prevention; Everyday Health. Retrieved 27 August, 2020, from https://www.everydayhealth.com/narcissism/

Lancer, J.D. (2018). Toxic Relationships, Psychology Today: Gaslighting. Retrieved on 27 August, 2020, from https://www.psychologytoday.com/us/blog/toxic-relationships

Lancer, D. (2020). What is Narcissism?; Psych Central. Retrieved on September 2, 2020 from https://psychcentral.com/lib/what-is-narcissistic-abuse/

Mandal, A. (2019). What is Narcissism? News Medical Life Sciences. Retrieved on 27 August, 2020, from https://www.news-medical.net/health/What-is-Narcissism.aspx

Mayo Clinic. (n. d.). Narcissistic Personality Disorder. Retrieved on 27 August, 2020, from https://www.mayoclinic.org/diseases-conditions/narcissistic-personality-disorder/symptoms-causes/syc-20366662

Miller, A.M. (2018). 10 Myths about Narcissism. Retrieved on 30 August, 2020, from https://health.usnews.com/wellness/mind/articles/2018-07-23/10-myths-about-narcissism

Miller, K. (2019). Avoid All 6 Types of Narcissists—but Mental-Health Pros Say One Type Is Especially Damaging; Well + Good. Retrieved on August 31, 2020, from https://www.wellandgood.com/types-of-narcissists/

Moore, A. (2020). 8 Types Of Narcissists & How To Distinguish Them; mbgmindfulness. Retrieved on August 31, 2020, from https://www.mindbodygreen.com/articles/types-of-narcissists

Myupchar. (2019). What is narcissistic abuse and how does it affect its victims; Firstpost. Retrieved on September 2, 2020, from https://www.firstpost.com/what-is-narcissistic-abuse-and-how-does-it-affect-its-victims

Nall R. (2020). Medical NewsToday: What are the long-term effects of gaslighting? Medically reviewed by Litner, J. Retrieved on 30 August, 2020, from https://www.medicalnewstoday.com/articles/long-term-effects-of-gaslighting

Pietrangelo, A. (2018). How to Recognise the Signs of Mental and Emotional Abuse; Health line. Retrieved on September 5, 2020, from https://www.healthline.com/health/signs-of-mental-abuse

Pietrangelo, A. (2019). What Are the Short- and Long-Term Effects of Emotional Abuse?; Healthline. Retrieved on September 5, 2020, from

https://www.healthline.com/health/mental-health/effects-of-emotional-abuse

Powell ND, Sloan EK, Bailey MT, et al. (2013). Social stress up-regulates inflammatory gene expression in the leukocyte transcriptome via β-adrenergic induction of myelopoiesis. Proc Natl Acad Sci U S A. 2013;110(41):16574-16579. doi:10.1073/pnas.1310655110

Raypole, C. (2020a). 12 Signs You've Experienced Narcissistic Abuse (Plus How to Get Help); Healthline. Retrieved on September 1, 2020, from https://www.healthline.com/health/narcissistic-victim-syndrome

Raypole, C. (2020b). 9 Tips for Narcissistic Abuse Recovery; Healthline. Retrieved on September 2, 2020, from https://www.healthline.com/health/mental-health/9-tips-for-narcissistic-abuse-recovery

Rhodewalt, F. (2020). Narcissism; Britannica. Retrieved on 27 August, 2020, from https://www.britannica.com/science/narcissism

Robin, S. (2007). The Gaslight Effect: How to spot and survive the hidden manipulation others use to control your life. Retrieved on 27 August, 2020, from www.penguinrandomhouse.com/books/the-gaslight-effect-by-dr-robin-stern

Robin, S. (2011). Gaslighting effect: Don't be afraid to speak your truth. Retrieved on 27 August, 2020, from www.huffpost.com/entry/gaslight-effect-dont-be-afraid

Robin S. (2018). Gaslighting in Relationships: How to spot it and shut it. Retrieved on 27 August, 2020, from www.vox.com/platform/amp/first-person/Gaslighting in Relationships: How to spot it and shut it

Rogoza R., Żemojtel-Piotrowska M., Kwiatkowska M.M., and Kwiatkowska K. (2018). The Bright, the Dark, and the Blue Face of Narcissism: The Spectrum of Narcissism in Its Relations to the Metatraits of Personality, Self-Esteem, and the Nomological Network of Shyness, Loneliness, and Empathy. Front. Psychol. 9:343. doi: 10.3389/fpsyg.2018.00343

Sarkis, S. (2020). How To Know If You're Dealing With Gaslighting At Work; mbgmindfulness. Retrieved on September 9, 2020, from https://www.mindbodygreen.com/articles/gaslighting-at-work-examples-and-what-to-do-about-it

Shipp, L. (2020). What Is Gaslighting? Psychology, Effects On Relationships, And Treatment; Medically Reviewed by Horn, A. Retrieved on 27 August, 2020, from https://www.regain.us/advice/psychology/what-is-gaslighting-psychology-effects-on-relationships-and-treatment/

Slavich GM, Irwin MR. (2014). From stress to inflammation and major depressive disorder: a social signal transduction theory of depression. Psychol Bull. 2014;140(3):774-815. doi:10.1037/a0035302

Smith, S. (2020). Deal with Gaslighting – How to Deal with Gaslighting in 6 Easy Steps; Marriage.com. Retrieved on September 9, 2020, from https://www.marriage.com/advice/mental-health/how-to-deal-with-gaslighting/

Stebar, C. (2019). 9 Signs Your Mom May Be Gaslighting You, According To Experts; Bustle. Retrieved on September 9, 2020, from https://www.bustle.com/p/is-my-mother-gaslighting-me-9-signs-of-this-manipulation-tactic-according-to-experts-18551081

Tracy, N. (2012a). Emotional Abuse: Definitions, Signs, Symptoms, Examples, HealthyPlace. Retrieved on September 3, 2020, from https://www.healthyplace.com/emotional-abuse-definitions-signs-symptoms-examples

Tracy, N. (2012b). Psychological Abuse: Definition, Signs and Symptoms, HealthyPlace. Retrieved on September 4, 2020, from https://www.healthyplace.com/psychological-abuse-definition-signs-and-symptoms

Tracy, N. (n. d.). Gaslighting Definition, Techniques and Being Gaslighted, HealthyPlace. Retrieved on 28 August, 2020, from http://www.healthyplace.com/abuse/emotional-psychological-abuse/gaslighting-definition-techniques-and-being-gaslighted

Valecha, K. (2020). How To Deal With A Gaslighting Spouse?; Bonobology. Retrieved on September 9, 2020, from https://www.bonobology.com/how-to-deal-with-a-gaslighting-spouse/

White-Cummings, C. (2016). Toxic Relationships: A Serious Threat to Mental Health. Retrieved on September 2, 2020, from

https://ourselvesblack.com/journal/2016/8/6/o7cqjfs4o2b61y12ujl 1u96otlb6ua

Wolff, C. (2018). 9 Subtle Differences Between Being A Narcissist Vs. Just Being Self-Centered; Bustle. Retrieved on August 28, 2020, from https://www.bustle.com/p/9-subtle-differences-between-being-a-narcissist-vs-just-being-self-centered-8968106

Made in United States
Cleveland, OH
25 February 2025

14681145R00113